MORE
STORIES FROM
MAMA'S BABIES
PET SITTING

GARRY WHITE

Foreward by Vicky Owens McGrath DVM

HALEYA
publishing
.COM

FOR ALL THE PETS WE SIT FOR THANK YOU FOR THE MEMORIES.

Hello and welcome to my second book of pet sitting stories. For over twenty years my wife Teresa owned Mama's Babies Pet Sitting. She and I worked together in the business. This book is more stories of experiences and adventues we had pet sitting. Pet Sitting was not the career I originally picked for myself. But the Universe had it all planned out before I just didn't know. The truth is I feel blessed to have been called where I was able to give pets and animals the care they needed and help them feel at peace. Teresa and I did it for the pets they came first before anyone or anything else. Read and enjoy More Stories From Mama's Babies Pet Sitting.

FORWARD

Foreword for More Stories from Mama's Babies Pet Sitting

I was honored to be asked to write a foreword for this book of stories from Garry and Teresa White's adventures while pet sitting. Having known Garry and Teresa for many years, I know how dedicated and compassionate they are toward the pets in their care. Stepping into the world of animal care provides lots of opportunity for great stories. Garry reminds us in this book that pet sitting is not just a job, but a collection of big and small moments that will stay with you.

Pet sitting is much more than just filling food bowls and walking dogs. It is taking on the role of a trusted companion when pet owners are working or traveling. It requires showing up for early mornings and late evenings, administering medications, walking in all kinds of weather, cleaning litter boxes, and giving unconditional love. Garry and Teresa have obviously formed bonds with so many different animals over their career. The patience, kindness, and respect for their pet clients are evident through all the memories Garry shares in this book.

I hope you enjoy this glimpse into the escapades of pet sitting that Garry relays in this book!

Vicky Owens McGrath, DVM

INTERVIEW

A girl called and said she was a student of a professor who was a client of Teresa's. The professor told her to call us for an interview for a class project.

I'm sorry I don't remember the girl's name, but she did a great job. Not everyone can conduct an interview, but this girl did great. She was scheduled for a 30-minute interview, but we ended up giving her 45 minutes. When the interview was over, we stayed and talked with her. She showed us her sugar glider and two guinea pigs. It was a fun day for all.

JERRY

Jerry is a cat who loved listening to Teresa read. When we go in, Teresa fixes his food, I clean his litter box, and one of us gets fresh water.

After we finish everything, Teresa goes into the living room, sits on the couch, and starts reading out loud. Jerry eats, and when he's done, he comes into the living room, lies at Teresa's feet, and listens to her read until he goes to sleep.
We sat for Jerry for a month, and during that time, Teresa read two or three thick books to him.

The lady called again to set up more pet sitting for Jerry. She told Teresa, "Jerry wants to see his Aunt Teresa."

BELL AND RAISIN

Bell and Raisin are hunting dogs. They have a huge cage behind the house that's attached to the garage, so they can go in and out through a doggie door.

The first thing Teresa does is let Bell and Raisin out—and that's when the fun begins. They shoot out of their cage and go running across the yard. They have a huge backyard with plenty of space to run, with hills and woods all around the property.

They're a laugh a minute to watch—running up one hill, back down, then around the yard, up another hill, down again, and across to the edge of the woods. And they do all of this at full speed!

My job is to watch and make sure they come back. While I'm doing that, Teresa is fixing their food, getting fresh water, and cleaning their cage.

When they get back from their run (and after doing their business), Teresa has their food ready. They go into their cage to eat. It's so funny—they eat dry food, but Bell has her own routine. She takes her front paw, flips her bowl, spills the food all over the floor, and then eats it off the floor. That's just the way she does it. It's her thing.

CASHEW

Cashew was a sweetheart of a cat. She was an indoor cat. The couple who had her called, asking for pet sitting — it was Christmas time, and they were going to see family. Cashew got out of the house. They couldn't find her. They kept waiting for her to come home. They looked and waited, but no Cashew. So they called us, saying they'd be staying home — because if Cashew came back, she wouldn't be able to get in. But she showed up in time for them to take their trip! They called us back, and we took care of Cashew that Christmas. We had a lot of respect for the couple — they put their pet first.

After Cashew passed away, the couple got two new cats. They were indoor-outdoor cats, so the couple opened a kitchen window so the cats could go in and out as they pleased. It was good and bad—sometimes they weren't home when we came by, and we like to see the pets so we know they're okay. We did the job, and when the couple got home, they called to thank us and told us the cats were home and doing fine

PIPER

Piper is a little Poodle. We have known Piper for a long time, but we never sat for her. This is a sad-happy story. We were talking with Piper's owner, and she was telling us that Piper was going to have surgery. As bad as it felt hearing this, I felt so good when her owner said they had canceled some of their vacations to pay for Piper's surgery. "We'll just go later," she said.

It's great to know people feel that way about their pets—like Cashew's family. Piper came through the surgery with flying colors.

HENRY

I told you about Betty and The Boys in the first book. They have a new addition to the family: Henry—and yes, he's a Cavalier King Charles Spaniel. He is the most loving little guy—you can't love him enough. Now when Teresa and I sit down to pet, we each get two dogs.

YOU HAVE MY CHAIR

We had just finished a job and had some extra time. We were taking care of two cats, Chester and Meme. Teresa had a new book she was reading—it was one of those books you just don't want to put down, so every free minute she would read. Teresa said, "Come sit down and I'll read to you and the cats."

There were just two chairs in the small room. I sat in one, and Teresa sat in the other. I didn't get to sit long—Chester came in and climbed up on me.
I thought he wanted to sit in my lap.
Nope. He wanted the chair. So I
got up, and yes, he got the chair.

As he listened to Teresa read,
he started licking himself,
as cats do. Then he fell off
the chair onto the floor.
Back up into the chair
he went. No, I never
got the chair back.

4

CHARLIE

I told you about Lola in the first book of these ongoing stories. Lola is a Labradoodle. Now, I want to introduce you to Charlie. We met Charlie's owner before she even had Charlie. She's a friend of Lola's owner. One day, we were sitting for Lola and this girl was there. She told us she was getting a dog and wanted us to sit for him. She said, "I've heard great things about you guys from Lola's owner."

A few weeks later, we were sitting for Lola again when there was a knock at the front door. I answered it—it was the same girl, and she was holding a baby Goldendoodle. She said, "I want you guys to meet Charlie." We met Charlie at just 7 weeks old.

The following week, we went to her house and completed the sitting contract for Charlie. Then came the day we were scheduled to sit for him. The first thing we did was get Charlie out of his crate and take him outside to go potty. The funny thing was, there was a little ditch across the backyard— just the right size for Charlie to fit in. He walked right over, laid down in it, and relaxed. I got him out of the ditch and told him to go potty. We went back inside and played for a bit. Then Charlie climbed onto the couch, laid down next to Teresa, tucked his head behind the pillows, and went to sleep. We sat for Charlie again about three weeks later. You wouldn't believe how much he had grown—he was a big boy, full of energy!

A really fun day was when we got to sit for Lola and Charlie together at Lola's house. We had a ball! They played and wrestled—they're the best of friends. In between their wrestling matches, we managed to sneak in some petting. We're hoping we get to sit for them together again. I call them the Doodlebop Dogs.

COCOA, BLITZ a.k.a. DOC, AND DIXIE

Cocoa is a brown Labrador Retriever—a really laid-back boy. "Feed me, pet me, I'm good!" That was his attitude. So we'd feed him, give him a few pets, and then he'd lie down and go right to sleep.

Then there's Blitz, a French Pointer. Blitz was a good boy —but busy. He was never still, always on the go in the house, in the yard, around and around, always moving. And he always had a bone in his mouth. I called him "Doc" because I'm a huge Doc Severinsen fan. I told Teresa that with his bone, he looked like Doc with his trumpet.

Cocoa and Blitz lived in the basement and garage. They had a doggie door from the garage to the yard, and another doggie door from the garage to the basement. It worked great—until a storm hit. Blitz did not like storms. When one rolled in, he wanted to be upstairs where there were people.

One day, the couple wasn't home. They sometimes let the dogs upstairs when they were around, but this time they were out. A storm came up, and Blitz went up the steps to the basement door. It was locked. He couldn't get in. In trying to open the door, Blitz mashed the doorknob flat— with his teeth. I wish Teresa and I could have kept that doorknob.

Blitz, a.k.a. Doc, passed away in 2016. After Blitz passed, the couple got Dixie—a Pitbull as white as snow and sweet as sugar. She was just like Cocoa. All she asked was: feed me, pet me. There was a fence around the yard. Whether it was Cocoa and Blitz or Cocoa and Dixie, they would always meet us at the fence. We had to pet them before going into the house.

The couple eventually moved to another state, so Cocoa and Dixie had to move too. That's the great thing about Teresa taking pictures of the pets—we get to keep them forever.

AMBER, LUKE, KATERI, AND JORDAN

Amber was a diabetic cat who didn't like taking her shot. Up until that time, we had never been asked to give any pet a shot. Teresa was naturally a little nervous—as we all are with something new. But the girl with the cat said, "You can do it."

She handed Teresa a syringe, a needle, and an orange. "Take this home and practice," she said. Teresa did—and then had me try.

When it came time to give Amber her shot, Amber ran. She wouldn't stay still, so Teresa asked me if I could do it. Okay —first time for everything. Now I had to hit a moving target. And I did.

There were three more cats in the family. Luke was the only male. He was a gentle, mannerly fellow.

Kateri was a black tortoiseshell, and not one you could pet. She only liked her mama.

Jordan was the youngest and the most loving. After everyone else passed away, she was the only cat left—and she couldn't love you enough.

SALLY AND HELEN

Sally loves to go for walks. She doesn't want anyone else on her street—people or dogs. That's a no-no!

Sally is a sweetheart of a dog. She's 15 years old, but you'd never guess it—she acts like a puppy. It's so much fun to watch her when we take her for walks.

She'll take a little petting, then it's off to a place where she can be alone. That's just her.

Helen is a sweetheart of a cat. She'll let you pet her a little at times, but mostly it's just: feed me and go on your way. Helen is an outside cat when we keep her. I think she goes inside when her owner is home, but we're told not to let her in—because it's hard to get her back out.

It's okay for her to be outside. They live in a good neighborhood, so Helen is safe.

ANDI

Andi is a Goldendoodle. She is a loving girl. It was raining the first time we sat for her. We took her out to potty—she peed, and then she wanted to play. Rain meant nothing. Then she got the puppy crazies—she was just two months old. I'm trying to get her back in the house, and she's running around the backyard having a good time. Believe me, she could move. I don't know when I've had that much fun in the rain.

LOUIE

Louie is a red and white King Charles Spaniel. He belongs to a friend of Charlie's owner. One day, Charlie went out with his owner and her friend for the day, and they asked us to sit for Louie. We were happy they did! Louie was a great little guy. We went in, got him out of his crate, and Teresa took him outside to potty.

When they came back in, we gave Louie lots of love and attention. Teresa sat down on the couch to write her notes, and Louie climbed up onto the back of the couch and laid down behind me. He and I petted and played for a while. We hope we get to see Louie again—he's a wonderful little guy to sit for.

DEXTER

We met Dexter at a gas station. We had stopped to fill up the car. As I came out of the station after paying, I noticed Teresa pointing. Of course, I looked the wrong way at first, not knowing what she was pointing at. Then I saw him—a beautiful dog with his head sticking out of a car window.

I said hi to him and talked to him for a moment, then walked back to our car, where Teresa was pumping gas. As I was talking to him, his owner came out of the store. She pulled her car over to ours and told us his name was Dexter. He was a stunning Australian Shepherd. She told us Dexter loves people, and we told her we're pet sitters. We gave her one of our business cards. She mentioned she'd had bad experiences with boarding in the past. It was so fun meeting and petting Dexter. We hope we get to sit for him one day.

LUCY AND CHLOE

Lucy, a white Labrador Retriever, is the perfect way to start the morning. First thing when we arrive at Lucy and Chloe's, I take Lucy out to potty. It's so much fun to stand on the back deck and watch her run back and forth across the big backyard.

When she's done, she and I go back inside. I feed her, give her fresh water, and she eats. We pet a little, then she grabs her bone and lays down on her bed. I sit with her until it's time to go to the next job.

Chloe, a 2 lb Yorkie, thinks she's bigger than Lucy. She takes care of the house and property—she says she's the boss! Teresa handles Chloe's food, water, and potty pads. We both share in petting Lucy and Chloe. Chloe loves to give kisses. She and Lucy love everybody. I call them little hippie dogs because they love everyone.

MOZART AND SASHA

Mozart and Sasha were two of the sweetest little Dachshunds ever. Mozart was wirehaired. Sasha was shorthaired. We sat for Mozart and Sasha for a few years, then they moved away. We would go in, give them food and fresh water, then take them for long walks around the neighborhood. They lived in a nice part of town, so walking was no worry. They were fun to walk—never gave us any trouble. We have fun memories of Mozart and Sasha. After we got back from our walks, we would pet and pet and play on the floor.

GABBY, BLACKJACK, BROKER, TIGGER WOODS, JAI ALAI, AND MAVERICK

Let me tell you about a group of Boxers: all champion show dogs. We took them out one at a time—they couldn't go out together. That didn't work—if you did, they just wanted to play. It was so much fun. They were well-behaved and never gave us any trouble. We loved walking around and looking at their awards and trophies—they had them all over the house. We've done a lot of show dogs over the years. That's a world of its own.

MOLLY

Molly was a Boxer—so sweet and friendly, as Boxers are. We would put her leash on and take her for a walk. She was always a lady. She lived on the second floor of an apartment building and always walked gently down the steps. We were always on a happy cloud when we got a call to sit Molly.

EMILY ANNE

Emily Anne was a Yorkie and a sweetheart. She drank a lot of water, so we had to keep her bowl full. She had a fenced-in backyard. We'd walk around the yard with her—slowly. After her walk, we'd take her in, feed her, then pet her a little. She didn't care for much petting. At night, we would alternate the light for her—we didn't want to leave her in the dark. We only sat for Emily Anne a few times, but she was one you never forget.

BUCK AND BELLA

Buck and Bella were two 8-week-old Boxers—the sweetest, cutest little babies. Buck was the boy, Bella the girl. They came from a litter of eight.

We visited twice a day: once in the morning and once in the evening. We always got a hero's welcome from Buck and Bella. We'd take them outside first thing. They did great walking on a leash. Then we'd bring them back in and play. They were so funny—we had a ball.

After a few months, they moved away, but we still have great memories of those two pups.

ELSIE AND JOSIE

Elsie and Josie are sisters, but they are as different as day and night. Elsie is a sweet cat and loves to be petted. She and Teresa sit on the couch and pet. Elsie purrs, rubs, and climbs on Teresa. They're best buds.

Josie is not a sweet cat—she's more of a loner. She likes her space. She hisses and spits and runs under the bed when you try to pet her. I love to listen to Josie meow. She doesn't really meow— she squeaks. It's so quiet.

They are good babies to take care of. Pet Elsie, let Josie have her space, and all is good.

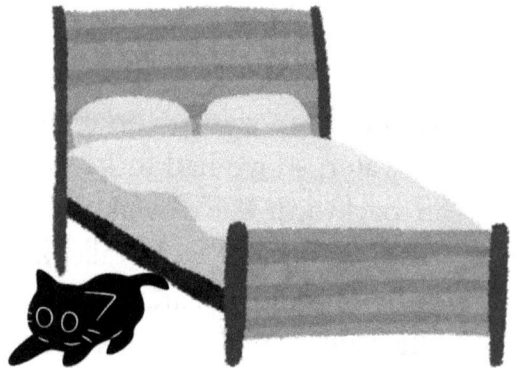

BOOMER, PIXIE, KAYLA, AND YODA

Boomer was an American Foxhound. Pixie was an Italian Greyhound. Kayla was an American Eskimo. Yoda was a Chipug. Boomer and Pixie were adopted from the Humane Society. They were both just babies—only a few months old —when they were adopted. They came home at the same time, which was a blessing for Boomer. He couldn't walk.

Pixie was much smaller than Boomer, but she took him under her wing, worked her magic, and taught him to walk. They were best friends for life.

Kayla—well, as I've said, you try not to have favorites. But Kayla always stood out to me. She was the sweetest girl and had the prettiest little face. I loved petting her—her hair was as soft as snow, and she was so loving. Kayla was my buddy. I always looked forward to seeing her. It hurt so much when she passed away.

Shortly after Kayla passed, Pixie passed away too. That's when Yoda came into the picture.

Yoda was a clown. He spent most of his time standing on his back legs. What he really loved was attention—he couldn't get enough of it.

The couple who had Boomer, Pixie, Kayla, and Yoda were so good to their babies. They took great care of them. Their house was set up more for the dogs than for themselves, and that always makes you feel good to see.

Teresa and I have a lot of happy memories with Boomer, Pixie, Kayla, and Yoda. They lived next to a golf course, and we would take them for walks around it. The dogs loved it, and the exercise was good for them—and for us. They never gave us any trouble and were always well-behaved.

HAKUTO

Hakuto was an apricot Poodle. His owner was a friend of the couple who had Boomer, Pixie, Kayla, and Yoda. At first, Hakuto would stay at their house when the couple and his owner went out of town.

Eventually, Hakuto's owner started traveling more often for work, so we began going to Hakuto's house to sit for him. First thing in the morning, we'd take him out to potty, then bring him back in, feed him, and give him fresh water. Hakuto was highly intelligent. You'd tell him to do something—and he'd do it.

I remember one night we were doing a pet-sitting job at a house a block over from Hakuto's. As we were leaving, walking down the driveway toward our car, we saw a girl walking a little dog. We didn't think anything of it—until all at once, the dog jerked loose from the girl and came running to us. It was Hakuto. We hadn't seen him in a while, but he had not forgotten us. So we sat down in the driveway and petted Hakuto.

FUNFETTI

We sat for a cat—the owner had him in the basement. It was nice down there. I always said he had his own apartment. Now Mr. Joey was a busy man. Teresa and I went in one day, and there was toilet paper wall to wall. There was a bathroom down there, and Mr. Joey had shredded the toilet paper on the roller—and another roll that was sitting on the back of the toilet. Mr. Joey walked around the basement so proud of himself. Teresa and I cleaned up the mess, laughing the whole time.

14

BUSTER

Buster was a Saint Bernard. He was the most loving dog ever —he loved Teresa and me from day one. We went to the house to complete the contract. Once everything was done, we started to leave. As we headed to the car, we looked down—and there was Buster, walking right beside us. He thought he was going home with us! The owners had to call him back into the house.

Another time, we were leaving and the garage door was up. As we walked out through the garage, we hit the button to close the door. Suddenly, we heard something. We looked back—Buster had run under the closing garage door. It hit him across the back and started to go back up. He was trying to follow us to the car again! Needless to say, we never got the chance to sit for Buster again. But we'll never forget him.

LUNA AND MUMU

Luna is a Lab mix. Mumu is a long-haired cat. We first met Luna and Mumu the day we went to complete the contract. Luna met us at the door, doing her little happy dance to welcome us into her home. She was so excited! First thing, we took Luna out into the backyard to potty—and that's when the real show began. It lasted all weekend. You've never seen anyone run like Luna. She was hilarious! Teresa and I had an absolute ball.

The whole weekend was a blast. Luna was a laugh a minute. Teresa eventually found Mumu hiding under the bed. His name may be Mumu, but he actually answers to "Kitty."

ANNIE

One of the most beautiful black cats ever. Annie is so sweet. She comes in, and she and Teresa pet. Annie is a loving cat. She loves to be petted—she never bites or scratches. Annie was not sure about me at first. She was so funny—she would just walk around or stand and look at me. That was the first trip. We went back on the third trip, and she and I became friends.

Annie has a little friend, Emma—a Shih-Tzu. Emma didn't stay home with Annie; she had other plans that week. We had a week to make friends, and Annie and I did it in two days. After we became friends, she and I would hang out together and pet. Teresa would get Annie's food together, Annie would eat, then she and Teresa would hang out together.

MEDITATION

Teresa and I had a cat of our own. She was an indoor cat.
I found it so funny—every morning I do meditation. Our cat always knew when I was meditating. She could be at the other end of the house, and as soon as I started, here she would come, rubbing back and forth on my hand. She was so funny. I'm sorry to say she passed away one evening. We miss her every day.

16

TOO MUCH ICE

A hard winter hit—sleet, snow, sleet, snow—it just kept coming and building up. But we had pet-sitting jobs to do. This one house had two cats. Everything was covered in ice. The front of the house had five, maybe six steps, and they were completely iced over with that winter mix. The steps were solid ice.

We thought, we'll just climb up, go in the house, take care of the cats—no problem. But no. We started to climb, got about halfway up—and slid right back down. We tried again. And again. Slid back down every time. We even tried using our feet to break the ice, making little holes for traction and trying to make mini steps. Still no luck. That ice was frozen solid. But the cats needed food and fresh water. So we kept trying. I just know—if any of the neighbors were watching—they got a good show.

That was one thing about us: when we were pet sitting, we got in the house and took care of the pets. If we couldn't get a door open, we'd go around the house, find a window, or check the doggie door. I've climbed in windows. Crawled through flaps. Whatever it took. Then I had an idea. I climbed up onto the end of the porch, walked across, and then laid down so I could reach Teresa. I started pulling her up. She couldn't help much—too slick—she just kept sliding back down. But we stayed with it. Finally got inside. Took care of the cats. All was good.

Leaving was easy—we went out the back door, which was on level ground. We would've come in that way to begin with, but we didn't have a key for the back. Another fun memory we still look back on and laugh.

CURLY, ELLA, AND MIDNIGHT

Midnight is a beautiful black cat that loves attention. The funny part is, when we first started, I could not remember his name. Then I started calling him Midnight Memphis to help me remember, and it worked!

Curly was a sweet baby dog. He was 13 when we started sitting for him, Ella, and Midnight. Curly didn't like petting —he liked to stay to himself. When we first started, we would take Curly and Ella for a morning walk. They did well at first, but then Curly just didn't feel like walking. So we would walk around in the backyard and let them do their business.

Curly passed away shortly after we started sitting for him, Ella, and Midnight. We are happy we got to know Curly and for the time we had with him.

Ella is a little toy Poodle. She was 14 when we started. Ella likes petting, so after our walk around the backyard, we would sit and pet Ella and Midnight.

Like Curly, Ella's health is not good now, so her owners take her with them when they go out of town.

We miss Curly and Ella. But we still have Midnight—a.k.a. Midnight Memphis.

Midnight
Memphis

MOCHA

Mocha, an American Shorthair, was a super sweet cat. She was so much fun—it was like a game. Every time we sat for her, we had to find her. She was skittish, and when she heard us coming in the house, she would hide. But once we found her and she saw it was us, she'd jump up on the bed, and she and Teresa would have their time together. Mocha and Teresa did really well together. Mocha never had much to do with me, but she was a real sweetheart.

MOUCHIE

Another beautiful black cat. She loves to listen to Teresa read. When Teresa starts reading, Mouchie lies close by. Next thing you know, she's asleep.

Mouchie loves going out early in the morning. She and Teresa talk. When it's raining, Mouchie wants to go out—Teresa says no. Mouchie talks back. It's fun to watch.

When we first get to Mouchie's, Teresa prepares her food and gets fresh water. After Mouchie eats, Teresa lets her outside. She stays out for a little while, then comes back in, eats a little more, and settles in to listen to Teresa read. Mouchie's name means "love," and it fits her. While Teresa is preparing her food, she and I sit on the living room floor and pet. Mouchie is a loving girl.

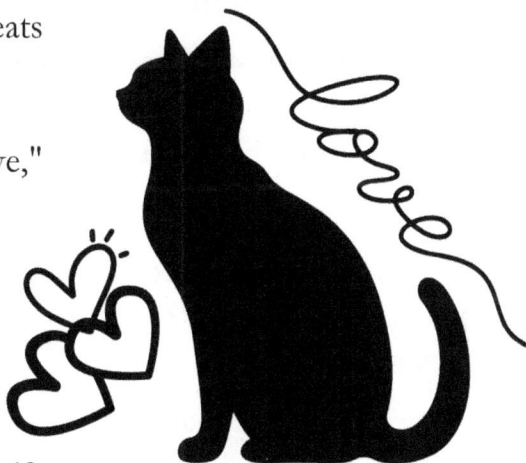

ACROBATIC DOGS

Mallie is a silver Labrador Retriever. Zoe is a Boxer. Two really sweet dogs with a lot of energy.

They use a lot of that energy to love you. They are inside dogs, and they use that energy when you let them out to potty. They never go down the steps—they leap from the back porch to the ground.

You have not lived until you've been standing in a backyard, turned around, and seen Mallie and Zoe coming through the air straight at you. That's the way to start a morning.
That's why I call them the Acrobatic Dogs.

RAIL FOR TERESA

Teresa has trouble going up and down steps. We have a client where we have to go down steps to get to the dogs, then back up to leave. The client had a camera to check on the dogs when they weren't home.

We went to take care of the dogs one weekend and noticed a new stair railing had been installed.

Teresa said, "This is great—I like this!"

Later, when the client called to let us know they were home, they asked Teresa, "How did you like the rail?"

Teresa replied, "It was great!"

They said, "We noticed you were having trouble with the steps, so we put the rail in for you."

Now that is appreciation.

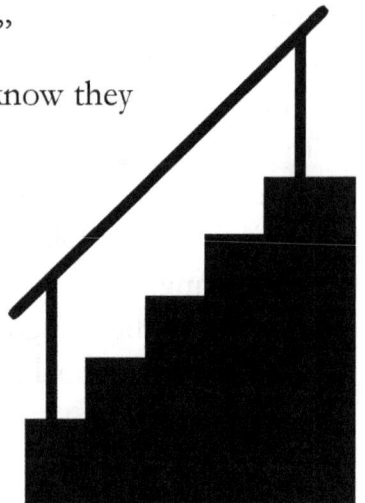

COCOA AND MOCHA

Cocoa is a Cocker Spaniel. Cocoa loves everyone—a friend to all. The couple who have Cocoa have done great with him. They tell him to sit—he does. They tell him to lie down —he does. They say, "Cocoa, say your prayers," and he lays flat on the floor, puts his head down between his front feet, and it looks as if he is praying.

I take Cocoa out to the courtyard first thing in the morning to let him get some fresh air and do his business. We go back in the house, he gets a little food and fresh water. Then he and I go for a walk. Cocoa loves his morning walks. I never thought about him being so strong—until the first time I took him for a walk. He is a stout little guy.

Then there is Mocha—a sweetheart of a cat. She's a little fuzzball with four legs. She talks with a lisp. Teresa and I love to listen to Mocha talk.

Teresa takes care of Mocha's food, fresh water, and cleaning of her litter box. Once we get Cocoa and Mocha's needs met, we all sit down and Teresa reads to us. Cocoa, Mocha, and I love to listen to Teresa read. She always has a great book with her.

MAGGIE

Maggie was a black Labrador. She was a big girl with a big personality. We only saw Maggie occasionally. She loved to run, so the first thing we would do was take her out and let her run and play in the backyard. Maggie loved hugs, so when we went back in the house, she wanted to be petted and give and get lots of hugs. That was great, because we love to pet and give hugs.

PARKER AND CHARLIE

Parker was a Coonhound. Charlie was a long-haired beige cat. Parker was an outside dog. He was tied to a dog zipline in the side yard. I had to take him for a walk every day. I would hook his leash on him, unhook him from the line, and we were off. Parker and I would go across the yard, through the woods, with him going as hard as he could—spinning me like a top! But we always made it on our walks. After our walk, Parker and I would get back to the house. I'd hook him back on his chain, and then he and I would sit and catch our breath. Good memories with Parker.

Later, the people who had Parker and Charlie called again for pet sitting. They said they had moved—Parker didn't have to be tied anymore. He was running loose. We didn't know what we would find. But it was as if they had a brand-new dog. You have never seen a dog so calm. Parker came up to us wagging his tail, let us pet him, then went and lay down. We could not believe what we were seeing—Parker was a new dog. We were so happy for him.

Charlie was an inside-outside cat. He only had one eye, but you wouldn't know it watching him move around the yard.

 He was a sweet cat—very affectionate and loving. Charlie didn't have one mean bone in his body. Teresa took care of Charlie's food, water, and litter. We both handled the petting and spoiling of Parker and Charlie.

That's one of the big things about Mama's Babies Pet Sitting: We guarantee to spoil. Parker and Charlie have passed away, but we have great memories of them.

Guaranteed to **spoil!**

MAX

Max was a Chow mix. Max didn't like kids. The lady who had Max had grandkids that picked at him, and he had his own room with his toys. They would go get his toys, and he didn't like that.

Teresa is 4'10". The first night we were getting things together to leave, Max went in his room. Teresa walked to the door of Max's room—she just stepped inside the doorway. Max showed his teeth—he thought she was a kid. From that night until that job was done, I had to do everything for Max. He would not let Teresa do anything for him.

I think we only took care of Max that one week. He was a good boy—he just didn't like kids. Everything was cool until he got the idea Teresa was a kid. No, no, no—can't have that kid around doing things for me.

NO KIDS ALLOWED

HARLEY, CASEY, AND LUCKY

Harley, Casey, and Lucky were three Sheepdogs. They were pretty uneventful—but they were good babies. It was so much fun taking care of them. I love Sheepdogs and getting to work with them and see how smart they are was such a joy. And of course—I love all that hair! We fed them, took them out to potty, then Harley, Casey, Lucky, Teresa, and I would all hang out together and just pet and relax.

SHELBY

Shelby was a brown Labrador Retriever. She always did a little dance and had a smile on her face. She'd even show her teeth. That smile scared some people at first, but in reality, she was just happy to see you. Showing her teeth was her way of saying hello.

Shelby loved to take walks—long walks—the longer, the better. She never gave us any trouble. She was always sweet and easygoing. Shelby was an outside girl, so her owners would leave the garage door open just enough for her to go in and out.

When we arrived at her house, she would come out of the garage walking stiff-legged, with her front toes spread out and her teeth showing.

She was a funny girl who loved everyone and had her own unique way of showing it. It scared some people when she showed her teeth—they didn't understand it was just her way of saying hello. We loved her, and she loved us. It was a sad day when Shelby passed away.

NUGGET

We took care of a little Yorkie—his name was Nugget. The little guy was blind, but you would never have known it, watching him get around inside the house.

We only sat for Nugget twice. The man who had Nugget called, asking us to sit again, but some trouble came up with his trip. We never heard from Nugget again.

Nugget was a perfect name for him—he was gold. Nugget was one sweet little guy. We will never forget him.

BISCUIT

Biscuit was a Boston Terrier. Most pets meet us at the door. Biscuit was always standing on the couch—after we got in the house, she would jump down and come see us. She was the most loving little girl; she couldn't love you enough.

She was full of mischief. Teresa and I would sit on the couch, and she would run back and forth across the couch and over us. She would jump up on us and lick us in the face.

I would take her out; Teresa would fix her food and water. Biscuit loved snow—anytime she went out and it was snowing, she was in seventh heaven.

HANZ

Hanz was a German Shepherd. A big boy—but a gentle giant. He was kept in a pen in the backyard, which was fenced in. When we came over, we would let Hanz out so we could play. He would come out full force, ready to have fun. Teresa or I would throw a ball, and Hanz would run, get the ball, and bring it back to one of us to throw again. We believe he would have done that for hours if time had permitted.

Hanz was always happy. We never saw him get upset or try to hurt anyone. We sat for Hanz for several years. He has now passed away and left a hole in our hearts.

BEN AND OLIVER

Ben was a black and white long hair cat. His full name is Benjamin Franklin—named after the man on the hundred-dollar bill. We call him Ben for short. Oliver was a blond American Shorthair. Two of the sweetest cats ever. Ben is a laid-back boy. Petting is his thing—either you're petting him, or he's petting you.

Ben and Oliver live at a business office. There is a counter with cabinets underneath that runs along two walls of the office. Ben can open the cabinet doors, get inside, and somehow manage to close the door behind him—so you don't even know he's in there! We were told he did this, so we knew where to look for him—and sure enough, there he was.

Ben and Oliver have free run of the offices. Teresa takes Oliver into one of the rooms to give him his pill, then she lets Ben in and reads to them. Once I finish my jobs, I join them. They get more attention, and we get to spend time with them.

We care for Ben and Oliver on Tuesday and Thursday mornings. They are always a great way to start the day.

Where's Ben?

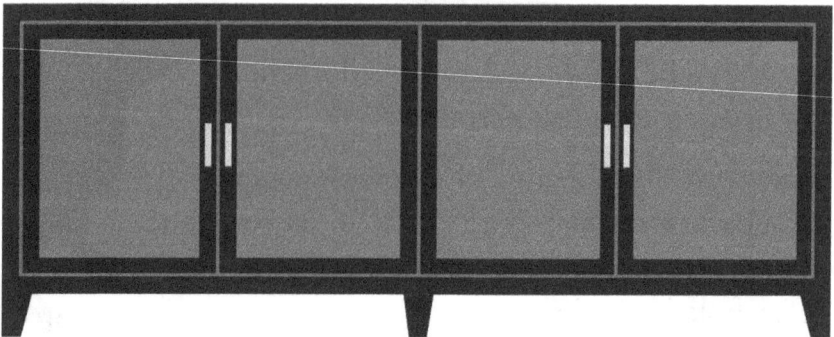

BEAR

Bear was a Goldendoodle. When we met Bear, he was about six months old—a ball of fire. He had so much energy! He could go from one end of the house to the other in record time—and this was not a small house. He had a big fenced-in backyard, so taking him out was easy. We would take him out first thing, then it was playtime. He loved to get on the back of the couch and howl at us, then run back and forth across the couch.

We took care of Bear again when he was nine months old. He was bigger—and a real trip. He and I would chase each other around the living room—around and around, making big circles. I would chase him, then he'd chase me. Then he would run and jump on Teresa. I think he wanted her to join the chase.

There was a part of the house he wasn't supposed to go. It had a sliding door. He figured out how to open it and get in. He never bothered anything—it was just, "I can do this." He was always getting into something. Get him out of one thing, turn around—he was into something else.

He was so much fun—you never knew what he'd do next. One time, Teresa was sitting, writing her notes. She put her ink pen down to check something on her schedule. She laid the pen in the middle of the dining table. Bear ran, grabbed the ink pen—and the race was on. He had pieces of ink pen all over the living room. We got it all back, and he was okay. Nothing was safe from Bear. He could get things from the middle of tables, off kitchen counters—he would take pillows off the couch and scatter them around the floor and chew on the corners. It kept us busy trying to stay one step ahead of him. We love to work with the busy pets.

SIR WILLIAM, MUSHU AND CURIOUS

Sir William, a Westie, and Mushu and Curious, both American Shorthairs, made quite the charming trio. Every day when we went in, Sir William and Mushu would always meet us at the door. Sir William wanted petting; Mushu wanted treats. It was funny—Sir William took up with me, and if Teresa went in first, Sir William would pass her and run to me.

After a little petting from me, he would run, jump up, and hit Teresa's leg as if to say hi, then run back to me. I would pet Sir William a little more, then go to the back of the house to get dry feed and fresh water for the cats and clean their potties.

Teresa would let Sir William out in the backyard—he had a nice big fenced-in yard to run in. Teresa would get fresh water and tuna fish for the cats and dry food for Sir William. They were a lunch run we did then—every day, seven days a week. Once we got everything done, it was a little more petting, then off to the next job.

RIVER, BROOKE, BLACKIE, KATIE, AND COCOA

River is a male Boston Terrier. Brooke is a female Boston Terrier. Blackie is a male American Shorthair. Katie is a female American Shorthair. Cocoa is a female Rocky Mountain Horse.

River was protective—of everything and everyone. But especially his owner. He thought it was his job to take care of her. And for a little guy, he did a great job taking care of her and the house.

Brooke, on the other hand, always wanted to be the center of attention. She was a busy girl—never still, always moving. The owner said she wanted to take River and Brooke to obedience classes, but she couldn't manage both at the same time. So she asked Teresa if she would take Brooke. Teresa said yes.

The funny part? One night we were all there at class, and Brooke just wouldn't do what she was told. She was giving Teresa a hard time. The guy running the class got frustrated and said, "I'll show her." He was confident he could get her to listen. Well, Brooke didn't do it for him either. If Brooke didn't want to do something—she didn't. Brooke was her own girl.

Blackie and Katie were barn cats. Teresa fed and took care of them. They were sweet—but not fans of being petted. Typical barn cat personalities.

And then there was Cocoa. Cocoa was one sweet girl. I always said we didn't sit horses—but Cocoa was the exception. There was no one else available, and the owner said, "It has to be you."

A FIRST

Just when you think you've seen everything, something new comes at you. I told you about Lola, a Labradoodle, in the first book. We were sitting for Lola again, doing two trips a day. On the morning trip, she was in a bedroom with the door closed. So when we went to leave, we put her back in the bedroom and closed the door.

Now, we don't know if Lola jumped and hit the door and the vibration caused the lock to trip, or if it was when I closed the door—but Lola was locked in. We had put her in the bedroom before with no problem. But, you know, first time for everything.

We went through the house checking over door frames, looking in drawers, trying to find a key to get Lola out. No luck. Teresa called Lola's owner—she brought a key and let Lola out. Strange day. A first, but a strange day.

ELSIE MAY

Elsie May is a Toy Poodle. There is not much you can say about Elsie May—or Miss M, as we call her.

She is pretty uneventful, but the first time I saw her, I had to put her in a book. She was the cutest little lady and so shy. She just lay on the back of the couch, wearing the cutest little outfit. When we pet her, she rolls up in a ball and hides her face. It's so cute.

Oh—Elsie May and Lola are cousins.

MUSIC IN THE AIR

For some reason, I had my guitar in the car. We were out pet sitting, and we had this one little dog—she was a sweetheart. I thought, I'll take my guitar in and play for her. I took it in, set the case on the floor, and she came over, looking and sniffing around. I took the guitar out of the case and set it on my lap — still, everything was fine.

And then I strummed the guitar—just one time. The little dog went running through the house, yelling. It was so funny. It was such a scary thing for her—she had never heard or seen anything like that before. I put it away so it didn't make any more sound. All was good again, and we were friends again.

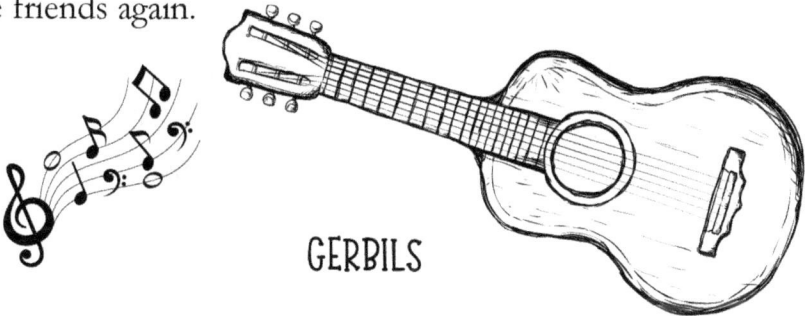

GERBILS

We did a job for a couple of years for a boy and girl who had two gerbils. Gerbils aren't real eventful—but still fun. The setup the boy and girl had was what made it special. The gerbils were in an aquarium that was designed so you could see them wherever they were. Their tunnels were arranged so you could watch them go through.

The boy and girl also had two dogs and two cats. We never sat for the dogs, and only a few times for the cats. Gerbil-sitting was our job. Then the boy and girl got jobs in another state, so off they went. I hated to see them go—I liked them a lot. It hurt, but that's how it goes.

CLOUDY

Cloudy is a toy poodle. Don't know why they call her Cloudy —she's a ray of sunshine! She has the best personality. She meets us at the door, all cheerful and happy.

First thing, we take her out for a walk. She shows us the way. Some days she wants to go up the street, other days down the street. Then, when she's ready, she turns around—and it's back to the house. Cloudy is a ray of sunshine.

ABBY AND BELL

Abby was a Shih Tzu. A little black and white fuzzball. It was fun taking care of Abby. She would walk through the house, and when she barked, she would say, "Bach Bach Puff Puff Bach Bach Puff Puff." Well, that's the way it sounded!

Then came Bell, a little gray Shih Tzu. She had a big basket of toys she would disappear in. She was so small, she got lost in it a lot.

It was fun listening to Abby walk around the house singing "Bach Bach," and looking for Bell when she'd get lost in the toy basket. We knew where she was, but sometimes we'd pretend we couldn't find her—just to make a fun game.

Abby and Bell have passed away, but the good and fun memories live on. When we talk about them, we always have a smile on our faces—and laughs follow.

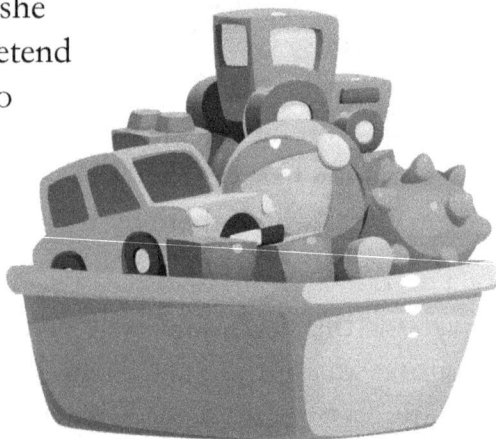

MERCY

Mercy was a Shih Tzu. The couple who had Mercy told us his story. They were driving down the road when they saw this little dog walking all alone. No one else was around, so they stopped and picked him up. They took him to the Humane Society to see if his owner would come looking for him. But no one ever did. After a week, the Humane Society called and told them, "If you want him, he's yours."

He was sick at the time, but with care from the veterinarian and lots of TLC from the couple, he got healthy and happy. They named him Mercy and gave him a good home. Mercy was always the best little guy. We would take him out to potty—he was so easy to walk. He had a big yard, and we'd walk and walk. Sometimes, if traffic was light, we'd take him around the neighborhood. He liked that. It was good for him —and for us too.

After our walks, we'd go back to the house and pet and play. We don't know why Mercy was out on his own that day, but in the end, he found a good home—and a family that loved him.

JAZZY

"Football girl," we called her. She loved to play with a ball bigger than her! She was a Yorkie, but it still took Teresa and me—yes, both of us—to take her out to potty and get her back in the house. There was a whole lot of girl in that little girl. The people who had Jazzy also had a cat named Ninja. She was an American Shorthair. Ninja was a sweet cat—we didn't see her much. She was a loner and stayed to herself.

ASKER

A beautiful gray and white American Shorthair. She is the sweetest cat and so funny. You'll be walking behind her, and she will just stop and lay down. Then you're dancing all over the room trying not to step on her.

Asker lives with us now. The lady who had her had a bad accident and couldn't take care of Asker anymore. Asker had nowhere to go. Teresa was talking to the lady on the phone, and the lady started talking about having Asker put down.

Teresa said, "No."

So she and I went to get Asker and took her to our house. She lives with us now. We didn't normally take pets home with us, but the thought of having Asker put down put a new light on things. Asker is still living with us. She is 19 years old now.

LOOKS LIKE A COMMERCIAL

Teresa was standing at the kitchen counter, putting dry food into a bowl to feed a Cavalier King Charles Spaniel we were sitting. I heard her say, "Looks like a commercial." I was on the other side of the kitchen and the counter from them. When I looked around, the little dog was jumping up— his head popping up and down behind the counter. Teresa was right —it did look like a commercial!

MARLEY

Marley, a poodle, was a funny little guy. He didn't like wet grass. When I took him out and it had rained, he let me know he was not happy. Now, if it was snow —he was fine. He loved snow.

Marley loved to listen to Teresa read. He would lay on the back of the couch behind her as she read.

The first time we kept him, we took care of him for a week. In that week, he took up with Teresa and me—and we with him. When we would get ready to leave, Marley wanted to go with us. That was the hard part—we couldn't take him home, but it would have been okay with him and with us.

NIKKI AND THOR

Nikki was a brown Labrador Retriever, and Thor was a mixed breed. They were so much fun and two of the best babies ever.

We would let them out in the backyard—it was such a joy watching them run and play around the yard. When they came back inside, we loved sitting with them. One would get on the couch with Teresa, and the other would curl up in the big chair with me.

They both loved to be petted. Nikki and Thor were the best-natured dogs you could ever meet. They never gave us any trouble and always made us feel welcome.

I think about them a lot—they were so sweet.

VELCRO THE CAT

Velcro was a diabetic cat. He had to have two insulin shots—one at 7 a.m. and one at 7 p.m. Teresa tried the first day, but he didn't like her. So I gave him his shots. He was the easiest cat I've ever given a shot to. We took care of him for a week. He never gave us any trouble, other than the fact that he just didn't like Teresa. She never did anything to him!

That's how it is in pet sitting. We go in on the first trip and feel the pets out—to see who they like. Some like men, some like women.

Velcro stayed in the upstairs bedroom. He had a nice big bed to lay on and a TV that played 24/7.
The only time he went downstairs was to eat or use the litter box. Other than the diabetes, Velcro had a great life—and he was happy.

VELCRO THE DOG

Velcro was a tiny Coton de Tulear. A woman was driving down the street when she saw a teenage boy kicking a little dog. She stopped, put the little dog in her car, and took her home. She named her Velcro because she stuck right up against her. When she got home, her three dogs didn't like Velcro, so she gave her to a friend—who was also a client of ours.

When we sat for Velcro the first time, Teresa and I sat down on the couch. Velcro got on the back of the couch and ran back and forth—pulling our hair! We sat for Velcro for maybe a year and a half. Then the lady had to move and couldn't take Velcro with her, so she gave her to another friend. Velcro has a great permanent home now.

CLAUDIE

We took care of a little dog named Claudie, a Poodle—she was a trip. The first thing we would do when we went in was Teresa would pick Claudie up. She had to carry her across the yard to the street, put her down, and then they would walk up the street until Claudie did her business. Then it was back to the house, with Teresa trailing along behind her. Claudie could move fast when she wanted to. Claudie was not very friendly. As soon as she and Teresa got back inside, it was hands off. She would take treats but no petting. But all in all, she was a sweet girl

SINGING THE BLUES

We were leaving a job one morning, and when we got to the car, we heard dogs yodeling. We stopped to see where it was coming from. It was coming from the house we had just left. We had already put the three dogs we were taking care of in their crates, so we went back in to see what the trouble was. No trouble —they were just laying in their crates, yodeling. I asked, "What's the trouble?"

They stopped and looked at me with a look like, "What?" Teresa called it singing the blues. And they were singing the blues. In pet sitting, no two days are the same. No two jobs are the same. That's one of the great things about the job.

37

ONCE IN A LIFETIME

Talk about seeing things you may never see again. We were on a pet sitting job. The couple we were sitting for had bought a new recliner and had put the old one out on the side of the street for trash pickup. I saw a car stop in front of the house. At first, when I saw a girl get out, I thought she was delivering packages. Then I saw her looking at the chair. I told Teresa, "There's a girl looking at the chair."

Then the show started. She was driving a hatchback. She ran around and around the chair, looking at it. Then she dragged it to the back of her car and opened the hatch. She took the back off the recliner and proceeded to put the seat in the back of the car. It didn't want to go. Then she started brushing the seat off with her hand. She got down and started smelling it. Teresa and I lost it. I haven't laughed that hard in a long time.

Again, she tried to put it in the car. It still didn't want to go. She started pulling stuff out of the car —a trash can, and I don't know what else—but it all went into the street to make room.

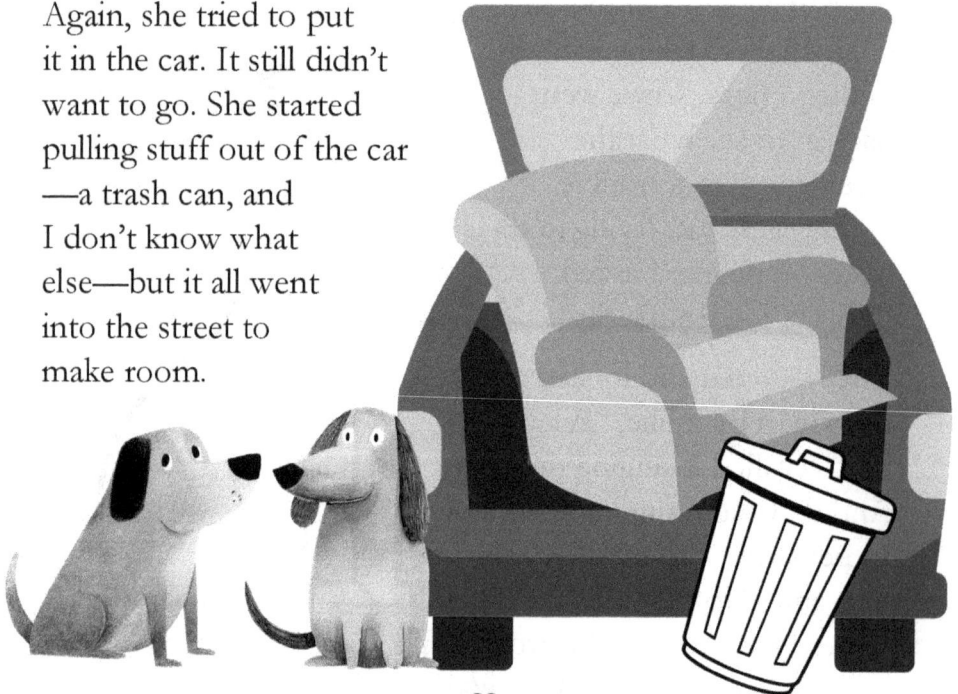

Then she was lifting and pushing, trying to get it in. She went around, got in the back seat—she had two dogs back there—put one in the front seat, then put the back of the chair in the back seat. I'm guessing she had done this a lot because she had work gloves that she put on.

She kept working until she got it in the car. If it got stuck, she would turn around and hit it with her butt. She had the whole car rocking, but she got it in and got the hatch closed. She got all the stuff she had put in the street back in the car, closed the doors, and off she went.

What?

AND MORE ONCE IN A LIFETIME

Talk about once in a lifetime! Teresa and I were on the interstate. We had just left a job and were driving home. We saw a car parked on the side of the road. The driver's side door was standing open, the window was down, and a macaw was sitting in the window. It was just sitting there, looking around. It was a beautiful bird with the most vibrant feathers, shining in the sun—so bright and colorful.

SNOW CATS

One of the coolest things we've seen while pet sitting: I've heard of snowmen—but never snow cats! The house next door to where we were pet sitting had made snow cats in their front yard. It was so cool. Another first and only for us.

HANK, SUSIE, JOSIE, AND NELLIE

Hank was a Coonhound. Susie was a Labrador Retriever. Josie and Nellie were American Shorthair cats. I would take Hank and Susie out. Teresa would feed Josie and Nellie, clean their potties, and give them fresh water. When Hank, Susie, and I came back in, I fed them.

Then it was time to play. Teresa and I had some great times running through the house playing with Hank, Susie, Josie, and Nellie—mostly Hank and Susie. Good times, good memories. I don't think the couple who had them would have liked it much, knowing we were running through their house. But oh well—the babies came first.

REX

Rex was a Shepherd mix. The first time we met Rex, he wasn't quite a year old but was full of energy. We had a great time with Rex. He always gave us a hero's welcome—jumping and barking. Rex had a great setup: a big fenced-in yard with a big dog house. Nothing but the best for Rex.

There were mixed feelings on the last day of our job—happy we got to meet Rex, sad that it was supposed to be a one-time thing. But when Rex's owners got home, they were so happy to see how good and happy he looked. They said they would call us again. We did sit for Rex one more time, but sad to say, we never got to see him again. In pet sitting, some jobs are short, some you may do for years—but they are all great jobs.

Hero's Welcome

BECKY

Becky was a 2-lb longhaired Chihuahua. You didn't get anything past Becky—she was smart and tough for a 2-lb Chihuahua who thought she was as big as a Mastiff.

We had to go to her house one day after a big snow. Her owner was shoveling the driveway, and Becky was out walking around like it was a summer day. She thought everything should be done on her time, and if it wasn't done to her liking, she'd tell you about it.

She didn't like to be held but would sit with you on the couch. Becky may have been small, but she was the boss of the house. What she said or wanted went. If she wanted something, she'd let you know — and you'd better do what she said.

Becky is gone now. She passed away, but she left happy memories.

TODD

We sat for a beautiful Collie. His name was Todd, and he was a sweet boy. There was a cattle farm that joined Todd's backyard. It was so fun to watch him run back and forth along the fence, barking at the cows. The cows would just stand and look at him as if to say, "For real, guy?"

When not playing with the cows, Todd loved to be petted. He was one of the sweetest dogs we've ever taken care of. We only sat for Todd once, but we will never forget him. We ran into Todd's owner a few years after we had sat for him. He told us that Todd had passed away.

LEIA, SKIPPER, AND SPARKY

They were three sweet dogs—pretty uneventful overall. We took them out first thing, let them potty, went back in, fed them, and then it was petting time. They loved being petted. Sparky sat on one couch with Teresa. Leia and Skipper sat on the other couch with me. Sometimes they would get in the floor and play with their toys.

The funny part was Sparky—he wasn't a people dog. But he liked me. An older gentleman who lived behind them told the owners when they got home, "You may need to watch Sparky. He just might go home with Garry." Now that's funny.

One evening, the owners came in, got some treats, and had the dogs dancing in circles in the middle of the kitchen. We saw a dog ballet that evening. Now that was cool.

BALLERINA GIRL

We sat for a dog—I can't tell you her name, because I don't know it. I just called her Ballerina Girl because she danced all the time. She danced all over the house.

She was a Karelian Bear Dog. We took care of her five days a week at lunch. So, we'd go at lunchtime… and dance with the Ballerina Girl.

Ballerina Girl has a good home now, but life didn't start out well for her. She had been with people who abused her. They didn't take care of her, they didn't feed her—and if they did, they fed her cat food. She didn't have a real home. The people who had her were unhoused and constantly on the move.

When I learned her backstory, I was so happy she had finally found a good home. She was so sweet—I don't know how anyone could be mean to her. Ballerina Girl is a ray of sunshine to everyone she meets.

LOLA

I told you about Lola in the first book, in the lunch run stories. Well, I have another little story about her. She has an inquiring mind.

I was sitting on the couch one day, and the next thing I knew, Lola was on the couch with me, picking at my pocket. I carry a pad and pencil with me for my writing. She got into my coat pocket, pulled out my writing stuff, and wanted to play with it. She was so good—she had it out before I even realized it! She was one funny little girl.

COCOA

The owner told me, "It has to be you. No one else would be good enough for Cocoa." Cocoa was a sweet girl—and funny, too. She'd be out in the field, and when she saw us drive up, she'd run to the fence, shaking her head and nickering. We'd go into the field, and she'd walk us to the barn like a little guide.

While Teresa fed Blackie and Katie, I'd get Cocoa some grain and a couple flakes of hay. If needed, I'd clean her stall. Cocoa was such a sweet, gentle girl. After she ate, we'd spend some time petting her. It hurt—big time—when she passed. But she'll live on in my heart forever.

CARTER

Carter was a Maltese. A little white fuzzy ball—the cutest little guy ever—with the best personality. He is so sweet when we take care of him. The funny part: the girl who has Carter was single when we first started sitting for him. Then she got married, and the guy she married—his last name is Carter. Now Carter's name is Carter Carter!

When we would go in, Teresa would take him out. I would get fresh food and water. When they came back in, Carter would eat, then we'd play and pet. When Carter got tired, he'd get on the couch or chair, lay down, and go to sleep. But he always knew when we were leaving. He'd wake up to bid us a fine farewel —and get a treat.

CAT FAMILY

We sat for a family of cats: Petie, Leo, Maggie, Sport, Marvin, Giselle, Clairese, and Moxie. We loved when they called—it was a fun job.

The first house they lived in was cool. It was two-story, great for a cat family. The dining room had a big bay window the cats would lay in. Sometimes Teresa would sit in that bay window, write her notes, and pet the cats. There was always one or two that sat with her.

The house had a big room upstairs that the people made into a den. We would sit there with the cats and watch TV. The second house they lived in was great for a cat family, too. It was a nice two-story, built in a circle. On the first floor, you could go from the living room all the way around and back again—the cats loved it. They had all kinds of running space. Upstairs were the bedrooms. The cats had fun up there—it was big and open, great for running and playing.

One night, Teresa and I were going to a concert at the university here. We couldn't find a parking spot. Their house was just off campus, so we went and asked if we could park in their driveway. As we were standing at the door talking to the lady of the house, Sport stood on the stairs looking at us. He never moved. I've always wished I knew what he was thinking.

The couple who had the cats retired, and the cats moved to another state. But we have our memories—no one can take them away.

JUST LIKE OLD TIMES

I told you about Sophie in the book—about her moving away and how it hurt. Well, she moved back! We went and saw her. She looked great—same Sophie. She wasn't alone this time. She had two little friends with her: Lola and Smokey. It was great seeing Sophie again. We got to be with her for a good, long visit.

Once a pet moves away, we usually don't see them again or sit for them again. But from time to time, it happens. This time it did. We got to sit for Sophie again—for a few days— and her new friends. Lola is a Maltese. Smokey is a Poodle.

Now Lola and Smokey were a trip! When we went back to sit for the three of them, Sophie was herself—quiet and sweet. Smokey barked and barked. He wasn't sure about us; he had only met us the night before. I understand—we were new to him.

Lola didn't bark at us—she howled at us. She was so funny. But all went well. We took them out to potty, then went back inside and petted. Well, we petted Sophie and Lola. Smokey didn't think that was an idea he wanted to get in on. Things were good when we left. Smokey was still not sure about us, but he was doing better.

It was great seeing Sophie and sitting for her again. Sophie will always be special to us.

LIKE THE GOOD

OLE DAYS

THE MOVE

We had one couple we had sat for over a few years. We had been talking about how we hadn't heard from them in a while. Then one day, they called needing pet sitting. Teresa told them we had been thinking about them. They told her they had moved to the country and were afraid we wouldn't come out that far—so they moved back to the city just so we could pet sit for them again.

JAKE

Jake was a white Labrador Retriever. We went three times a day to take him for a walk. Jake was getting older and having trouble with his hips. He needed help getting up, but he walked fine once he was on his feet. Teresa, Jake, and I would walk the yard, making two—sometimes three—rounds around the house to let him do his business and get some exercise. Jake walked slow because of his hips…or so we thought—until one morning a cat crossed the yard.

Jake saw the cat, and he was off! It was all we could do to keep up with him. "Jake, we didn't know you had it in you!" was all we could think.

Jake loved petting, so we would take some time after our walk to sit and pet him before going to the next job.

Jake has passed away, but he will always be a special memory.

WALTER AND MOLLY

Then Walter and Molly came into the picture. Walter was a Mini Aussie-Poodle mix. Molly was a Chihuahua. I told you about Naga, Samantha Lu, Celaena Rose, and Annabelle in the first book. Celaena Rose got a new home with a couple, and she has a great life—nothing but the best for Celaena Rose. Walter and Molly came to live with Naga, Samantha Lu, and Annabelle.

Walter was a skittish little guy. He had been abused, so he wasn't sure about anyone at first. But over time, he got better. Molly was her own person. She would get her own treats— you had to watch her! She was so funny.

As I've said, as a rule, we didn't take pets into our home. But we all know things can—and do—happen. One time, Walter and Molly's owner had an accident and needed some minor surgery. So Walter and Molly stayed at our house for a few days. Now that was fun. They were the sweetest babies—you almost forgot they were even there.

CLOVER

Clover was a Doberman mix. She was the cutest little thing— not even a year old. Clover came to live with the group but didn't stay long. She got sick and passed away.
The short time she was with us,
she left a lot of good memories.
She was so sweet and loved everybody
—and everybody loved her.

RUDY

I also talked about Rudy in the first book. We didn't see Rudy for a while—his owner's job changed, and he and Rudy moved.

But Rudy is back! Getting to see Rudy again was another happy time for us. He was still the same Rudy. We went back a couple days later and took Rudy for a walk. He was a gentleman, as always. When we got back to his house, we petted—Rudy loves petting. Rudy and Teresa are still best friends. Rudy still makes every step Teresa does.

LUCKY ME, LUCKY YOU

LUCKY NUMBER SEVEN

We got a call from a girl who said she had seven cats and needed pet sitting. Two were downstairs and five were upstairs. Downstairs were Oliver and Keke. She told us Keke didn't like men. But on the first day, Keke and I became friends. Oliver was one sweet cat—he loved to be petted. He and Keke would go upstairs when the door was open.

Upstairs, in one bedroom, we had Kiki and Rosy. In the other bedroom were Janet and her two baby kitties—Little Mama and Kyra. They were just two weeks old. So sweet! Eventually, they got adopted and went to their new homes. We still had the big cats upstairs who kept us entertained. And that left us with the lucky number five.

BRANDI, BRUSIER, SAMMY, TOTO, AND PUFFY

Sammy and Toto are two of the sweetest cats. Toto keeps to himself—he's a loner. You can visit with him, just don't stay too long. He values his privacy. Sammy is a laid-back girl. She walks around watching us. She enjoys a little petting, but when she's done, she simply walks away.

Brusier is a 3 lb Chihuahua who thinks he's as big as a St. Bernard. Brandi is a good girl. She was shy when we first started caring for her—she used to hide under the desk in the home office when we walked in. But with a few kind words and a little patience, she always comes around. Brandi, Teresa, Brusier, and I go out to the backyard so they can potty. Then it's back in the house—we feed them, give them some love and attention, and make sure everyone is content.

Then there's Puffy, a Bearded Dragon. Teresa takes care of him. She holds out a jar lid, and he eats mealworms and crunchies right from it. It's fun to watch! Bearded Dragons aren't very active, but they're neat pets.

STAR

We sat for one cat that was a trip. Her name was Star—she got that name because she loved to get up high and look down at you. Star didn't care for cat food. She wanted baked chicken and cake—no icing, just cake. And cheese—she loved cheese. When she got hungry, she would sit and stare at her food bowl. Never said a thing—just sat and stared. That was fun once we figured out what she was trying to tell us. She loved petting—we did a lot of that. Some pets are a little more of a challenge, but once we got a routine down, we had a lot of fun with Star.

REMY AND STORMY

We sat for a pair of rats named Remy and Stormy. They were good boys who loved their vegetables. They had a three-story cage. While Teresa cleaned the bottom floors, they would go to the top floor. Then they'd move down as she cleaned the top floor—like little gentlemen waiting their turn.

The owners had a girl staying at the house while they were away. She was a super nice person. Teresa and I really enjoyed talking with her. We had a lot of laughs together. Her name was Diana. Diana, Teresa, and I are still friends. Most people you meet at jobs aren't that friendly, but Diana was (and still is) a sweet, special person. With Remy and Stormy, and Diana making us feel so welcome, it turned out to be a great job with great memories.

MUIEL

Muiel was a black-and-white sweetheart of a cat. We'd go in, give her fresh food and water, clean the litter box, and Muiel would eat. Then it was time to pet. Muiel loved petting. The first day, she sat in Teresa's lap. The next day, she sat in mine. It went like that all week—every other day, Teresa then me. After some petting, Muiel would hop on the back of the couch and lie down. She loved watching the birds out the window.

Nothing ever bothered Muiel— she was just a cool cat. When she wasn't being petted, Muiel was great at entertaining herself. She had a lot of toys and plenty of birds to watch.

HOLIDAYS

People ask us about holidays. We didn't get holidays in pet sitting. You do holidays early or late—never on the day of. Weekends and holidays are when you make your money in pet sitting. So, if you want to be a pet sitter, you will be working weekends and holidays. If we wanted to do something, we did it on a weekday if possible, or in the off-season—fewer people that way.

When people asked, "Did you have a good holiday?" we would say, "Yes, we got to see a lot of little fuzzy faces." That's the truth—you can't have a better holiday than spending it with pets.

Another thing about pet sitting during the holidays: as we drove from job to job, we got to see all the decorations. Some were really beautiful... some, not so much.

We had a game we played at Christmas—"Who had the prettiest tree?" There was one tree that won one year, and it was a beautiful tree. We could not believe it when we walked into the house and saw it. It holds the record, and I don't ever see anyone topping that tree. It was 18 to 20 feet tall—this was a big house.

We never got to see the tree again. The man's job took the family to another state, and when they moved, his wife gave the Christmas tree away.

It was a beautiful tree. I'm so happy I took a mental picture. Then there was the pet sitting job in a house that had a Christmas tree that looked as if it should have been in a house of ill repute. That's another story for another day.

PUMPKIN

I told you about Honey, Sunny, and Cammy Jo in the first book. Well, they have a new member of the family now—Pumpkin. She's an orange and white American Shorthair cat. A neighbor lady had gotten Pumpkin, but she didn't really want her. She had gotten the kitten for her grandkids. When she was going out of town, she asked one of her neighbors—who happened to be a client of ours—to keep Pumpkin while she was away.

But that family had a trip planned for the same week, so they called us. And that's how we met Pumpkin. She was just 6 weeks old when we first met her.

When the neighbor lady got back from her trip, she called and asked the family if they wanted to keep Pumpkin. They said yes—they had wanted her all along. All of us were worried the neighbor lady wouldn't treat Pumpkin well since she hadn't wanted a cat to begin with. So that phone call was a blessing.

The funny part? Teresa is a big fan of cats. She's had her fair share—at one point, she had 24 cats! (And believe me, having 24 cats at one time can get interesting.) Teresa was so happy when the family called to say they were keeping Pumpkin.

TERESA WORKING SOLO

When Teresa first started the business, I was still working another job, so she did some jobs by herself. There was this one job—the dog was kept in the kitchen. The door was blocked off. That was the only room with tile, and it was a huge kitchen in a huge house.

When Teresa went in, the house was dark. She turned on the lights as she went. The dog—a big brown Labrador retriever —was clearly looking for a way out. Teresa told me the poor baby must have been spinning in a circle in the middle of the kitchen. The dog had diarrhea and had sprayed it as she went around.

Teresa said it took her over two hours to clean it up.
That's pet sitting—you never know from one job to the next what you'll walk into.

What A Mess!

SLEEPING CAT

We were sitting for a cat. We had everything done, so we thought we would sit down with her for a few minutes. Teresa kicked off her shoes.

We were talking, petting the cat, had the TV on, and were watching a little of it, when Teresa said, "Look!" The cat had laid across Teresa's shoes, put her head in one of them, and went to sleep. We wanted to laugh but were afraid we would wake her, so we laughed to ourselves. As I have said before, when you work with animals—things happen.

SIR WILLIAM, HONEY DEW, SIMBA, FRANKIE, AND EDGAR

Sir William was a West Highland Terrier. Honey Dew was a Calico. Simba was an orange and white cat—a big boy who loved to eat. Frankie was a little black cat with a shy personality.

They were an ongoing gig—we took care of them seven days a week at lunchtime. Sir William and I were best friends. He would always meet me at the door. When I came in, it was as if he hadn't seen me in six months.

Once I got inside, Honey Dew was always on the dining table. Then I was petting with both hands! You couldn't help but feel loved with the four of them. Before I could even cross the kitchen, Simba had to be petted.

Then there was Frankie. She was selective with who held and petted her, but Teresa and I never had any trouble. Frankie loved to climb—she climbed on everything in the house.

Most of the time when we went to the house, I would go in first. If Teresa tried to go in first, Sir William always tried to get around her to get to me. First thing Teresa did was give the cats their treats, then she would feed them.

Then came Edgar, a Border Terrier. He had been abused, so the family took him in and gave him a good home.
Edgar was all boy—out of one thing and into something else. He wasn't a bad boy, just busy.

One day, I had finished up and was waiting for Teresa to wrap up her job. I sat down on the couch. The TV was on—they always left it on for the pets. I was just sitting there watching when I felt something. I looked down—Sir William had his head on one knee, and Edgar had his head on my other knee. I thought: This is the job of all jobs.

55

BABY

We sat for a little dog named Baby. He was a Shih Tzu. The couple who had Baby lived next door to the wife's parents, and Baby loved going over to their house. When I would take him outside, he'd head straight for their door.

One time we were sitting Baby, and his people—and their parents—had gone out of town the same week. Baby would walk to their back door and stand there, waiting. I'd say, "Baby, they're not home." He'd look so pitiful.

Next time we went outside—same story. We always found Baby in the big chair in the living room. We'd go in, feed him, take him out, and then he was ready to sit back and watch TV. He loved sitting in the big chair with Teresa and watching television. He was the best little guy—never gave us any trouble.

Baby loved treats. Anytime, any hour—he was always ready for treats! His tail looked like feathers. It was so funny. It was pretty, but it really did look like feathers. We visited Baby three times a day. Morning, noon, and night—Baby was always the same little cool guy.

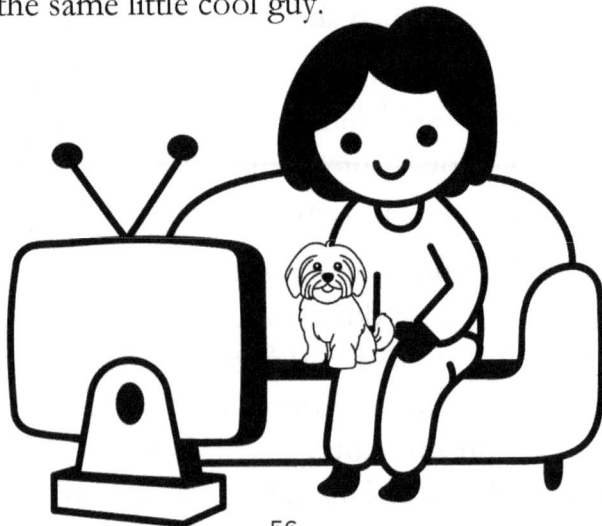

THE NOT-SO-GOOD SAMARITAN

We had been sitting for this lady for years. She had two cats —Sassy and Sebastian. They were beautiful and well-behaved. But this one time, the issue wasn't the cats—it was the not-so-good Samaritan next door.

It was Christmas, and we didn't have time to play games with this guy. As we were about to enter the apartment, he came out of his place next door—drunk—and told me he was supposed to take one of her cats for a walk.

I told him, "No."

He insisted: "She told me to take the cat for a walk. You go get a leash so I can take her cat for a walk."

I told him again, "No. She didn't tell me anything about someone taking her cat for a walk."

But he kept going: "You go get the leash." He was so drunk he didn't know what he was saying—or doing.

Eventually, I just walked inside and left him standing there.

At the time this happened, the lady only had the two cats— Sassy and Sebastian. Later on, she added three more: Nica, Jingles, and Jupiter.

COOKIE AND NELSON

Cookie was a Great Pyrenees. Nelson was a Golden Retriever. Cookie was a big girl—she got her name because she came from Cookeville, Tennessee. Nelson was a big boy too. Both were gentle and loving babies. They always met us at the driveway, and we always got a warm welcome from them. When it came time for us to leave, they always remembered: treats!

DOG FIGHTS

People ask, "You ever see any dog fights?" Let me tell you a couple stories. Once, we were having a nice, quiet morning. We had a few jobs—nothing big. We got to the second job and went into the house. There were four dogs at this one. We went in, and everything was cool. These were big dogs, but we'd never had any trouble out of them before. But you know, there's a first time for everything.

I had gone from the living room into the kitchen. Teresa was coming in behind me through the living room. I don't remember if I let the dog out of her cage in the living room or if Teresa did. I let one out of her cage in the kitchen. There were three in cages in the kitchen.

The one I let out went around the wall into the living room, saw the other dog with Teresa, and jumped her—and the fight was on. Teresa was yelling at them to stop. I was looking around for something to get them apart. I saw a bucket of water sitting just inside the kitchen door. I grabbed it and dumped it over their heads.

That did the trick.
It got them apart,
but the damage was done.
We put one back in her
cage. The one that was hurt—
we took her to the veterinarian
hospital and got her fixed up.

But this story has a happy ending.
The dog we took to the vet that day
got well, found a new home,
and now she's a princess.

AND MORE DOG FIGHTS

Then there was the job with eight dogs in the house. We got their food, and right in the middle of eating, six of them got into a fight.

Now here we were—Teresa and I with brooms—trying to get them apart. The floor was tile, and we were feeding them dry food. Dog bowls were flying through the air, dry food raining down on the tile like we were inside a didgeridoo.

We got things back together. The dogs ate, we went home, no one got hurt—and we had a good laugh. That's the life of pet sitting you never know from one job to the next what you will find or what will happen.

BASKETBALL AND TABLE

We sat for a woman who had five Great Danes. One of them loved to play basketball. He and I played a lot of basketball in his backyard—and he was pretty good at it Another of the Great Danes was so tall, we called him Table Dog. Teresa would lay her clipboard on his back as she wrote her notes. He was just the right height—it was perfect for her to stand and write comfortably.

Teresa would take the Danes out to potty one at a time. It was fun to watch her. Teresa is only 4'10", but she could handle those big dogs with no problem.

Another thing about Teresa that amazes me is how she remembers pets and their owners. She has such a memory for things that sometimes she blows my mind. But that's my wife.

WEWA AND HITCHKA

Wewa was a long-haired female cat. Hitchka was a gray, striped female cat. They were pretty calm, uneventful girls. But one funny thing happened—when we were going over the pet-sitting contract, we could tell the man had something he wanted to say.

We asked, "Is there something special we need to know?"
He hesitated, then said, "Well… at night, I cook Wewa a hot dog."

He went on to explain: "Take a hot dog, slice it down the middle in half, then slice those halves in half again, and then cube it. It has to be cooked in the oven—she won't eat it if it's microwaved. Cook it until it's brown and crispy. Then take it into the living room, put it on the bottom shelf of the end table by the couch, and sit on the couch so she can eat."

We said, "Okay, no big deal!"

The couple that had Wewa and Hitchka moved three or four times in the short time we sat for them. One of the houses had a driveway that went straight up—it was tricky to park on a good day. But guess what? It was winter—snow and ice everywhere. We parked at the bottom and walked up to the house. Eventually, Wewa and Hitchka moved to another state. We're happy for the memories we made with them.

TETLEY

Tetley was an American Shorthair. Her owner said her name was Tetley because she looked like a tea bag. She was a sweet cat, though she didn't like a lot of petting—she was very independent.

ALLEY AND HOBBS

Alley was a tortoiseshell cat. Hobbs was a calico cat. They had a great setup. There was a huge house, fixed up just for them with potties, beds, and all the room they could want to play. They had run of the whole house. Teresa would feed them in the kitchen. They even had placemats for their food bowls—and they ate different food, so she had to make sure the right food went on the right placemat, or they wouldn't eat.

It's always great to see pets that people really take care of. We've seen a lot of pets where people say, "Oh, we love our pets," but then when you go to take care of them, you think to yourself, Really?

But Alley and Hobbs were truly well taken care of. They had the best of everything, and everything was always there when they needed it.

Hobbs had a stool she sat on and looked out the window. When she was on her stool, you did not bother her— she would get you.

DON'T TOUCH!

WHERE DO I LIVE

There was this one couple we sat for—the wife's job took her out of town a lot. The husband always set up the pet sitting, so we mostly dealt with him. One time, while setting things up, he told us he had moved—but he didn't tell his wife. She was out of town at the time.

When the wife came home—well, so she thought—she discovered she didn't have a house. At least, not the one she thought. There was someone else living where she believed she lived. She tried to call her husband, but he was working, and she couldn't get ahold of him. So, she called us asking what was going on.

Teresa told her, "Your husband has moved." Teresa gave her the address to the new house, and then we met her there to let her in—she didn't have a key, of course.

You never know what a new day in pet sitting will bring. The couple had two cats. They were pretty uneventful—just routine food, water, and litter boxes. But the couple? They were the eventful ones.

MACEY

Macey was a Labrador Retriever—such a sweet girl. We sat for her many times. She never gave us any trouble. She loved everyone and was so easy to care for. We loved spending time with Macey.

Everything was set for us to sit for her in June. But in May, her owner called and told us Macey had passed away. We knew the day was coming. She had slowed down over the past few years.

BUTTERCUP, BERETTA, AND HEIDI

Buttercup is a Labrador Retriever. Beretta and Heidi are both Rottweilers. We sat for Buttercup and Beretta for eight or ten years. They were always good babies. But it didn't start out with sunshine and tail wags.

During the meet-and-greet, the owner was there, so everything went smoothly. But when we showed up on the first day of the actual job, Buttercup and Beretta met us at the door—and Beretta made it real clear: You're not coming in. So we got out the treats—treats are magic in pet sitting. We put treats through the door to Beretta, and all was good. We went in with more treats, and Beretta decided we were friends.

Then one day, the owner told us Beretta had cancer. We lost her to it not long after. Later, Heidi came into the picture—a real sweetheart. But a couple of years after Heidi joined the family, the owner moved away for a new job. It goes without saying—we'll never forget Buttercup, Beretta, and Heidi.

Yummy tasty TREATS

REAGAN AND DOOLEY

Reagan is a Shetland Sheepdog. Dooley is a Chocolate Labrador Retriever. Reagan was a pretty girl and a real sweetheart. She was a loving little thing—loved sitting with us and just being close. Dooley was loving too. She liked men more, so she would usually sit with me.

Then one night...I don't know what happened. They got into a fight. It seemed like Dooley jumped Reagan, and she came very close to killing her. Reagan was hurt pretty badly—but she pulled through and got okay.

After that, Dooley went to a new home. We sat for Reagan a few times after that. Then the girl who had Reagan got a new job, and that job took her away. We loved seeing those two. But now, we have our memories —and no one can take those away.

ALLEY

We sat for a cat named Alley. Alley ate canned food, but she had to have a different flavor every day—or she wouldn't eat. Her cans were lined up, so it was easy to pick a new one each day. Alley was diabetic and had to have two shots every day. She loved being petted. She and Teresa would sit and watch TV together and cuddle a lot.

It was a sad day when her owner called and told us Alley had passed away. Teresa always took pictures of all the pets we sat for, so we have our memories of all the babies. We are connected with them forever.

COOKIE, NELSON, TINKER, AND MITSO

We sat for a man who had four of the sweetest cats. They each had their own quirks, but we have great memories of them.

Tinker was so funny. When we walked into the house and she saw us, she would freeze like a statue. But as soon as we looked away—she was gone, running to hide under the bed. We always knew where she was, and she was fine.

Nelson was a shy little guy and a bit of a loner. He liked to stay under the couch. Teresa would feed him there. Tinker ate under the bed—they liked their own private "rooms."

Cookie—there's always one that stands out. Cookie was that one for me. There was an island in the middle of the kitchen. Cookie would sit on it, and she and I would sit and pet. We did that a lot. Cookie and I were best friends.

Mitso was a laid-back guy. A sweet cat—never made trouble for anyone.

Then one day, the man called and said he was moving and needed his house key back. So we went and saw the babies one last time.

That was hard. But we have years of memories—and we'll always keep them.

DEXTER

Dexter was a 35-lb cat. You didn't pet Dexter—you just let him be. He was not a friendly guy with anyone but his owner.

JEFF GORDON AND TINKER

Jeff Gordon is a Pomeranian, and Tinker is a Miniature Pinscher. We walked Jeff Gordon and Tinker regularly. They were easy to handle.

Jeff Gordon—I walked him. He and I just went right along, no problem. Tinker was a little different. She was skittish, a little unsure. She had been abused before, so she scared easily. She'd walk a few steps, then turn back a few steps. Teresa and Tinker were always behind us, taking their time. Tinker was never a bad girl—just not sure about everything. We sat for them for several years, and they never gave us any real trouble.

I never got to pet Tinker—unless Teresa was holding her. But Tinker was a sweet baby. It was so funny when we were walking she always watched me. Bless her heart she was just never sure. The people who abused her it's your Karma.

THE DOGS LIKED THEM

We set up a pet sitting job with a lady. She had two dogs. She gave us a key and went off on holiday with her family. When she got back, she told us she had been telling her family about us taking care of her dogs.

Her son said, "Mom, you gave those people a key to your house and left?!" She told him, "Well the dogs liked them."

UNFORGETTABLE

We had been working around the clock for days. We were going down Interstate 65, heading home to get some sleep. Next thing we know, Teresa and I both woke up—we had both fallen asleep and missed our exit.

We had to drive to the next city before we could turn around. Getting there and back added another hour on the road. If we had made our exit, we would have been home in five minutes or so.

Pet sitting can be an adventure—because we also missed a concrete pillar as we went through an underpass. Yes, we knew guardian angels were watching over us.

SYDNEY AND TAZ

Sydney is a Boxer mix. Taz is a Lab mix. Sydney loved being petted. She would sit with you as long as you wanted to pet her. Taz loved to play ball. He would play as long as you could hold out—Taz never tired out. The only thing he didn't like was giving the ball back!

We loved taking them out. They had a big backyard, and it was fun watching them play. The yard was fenced, but we had to watch Taz—he could, and would, get through the fence. He was a skinny little guy.

LARGE FAMILY

There were 2 cats, 2 rabbits, 5 dogs, and 3 guinea pigs.

Cats – Misty and Fancy (American Shorthairs)
Misty loved everybody and loved being petted. Fancy was a shy little girl. She would stand at the top of the stairs looking down on us. When we would go up, she would hide.

Dogs – Daisy, Jack, Buddy, Louie, and Brownie
Daisy is a Yorkie. The smallest of the crew but the boss of all. Jack is a Labrador Retriever. He was a friend to everyone, loved being around people, and had to be in the middle of everything. He was a funny guy. Buddy, Louie, and Brownie are Husky/Basset Hound mixes. All three loved petting. Their motto: "Just feed us, take us to potty, then pet us. That's all we ask."

Rabbits – Lily and Honey Bun
They had a big cage in the garage and a great setup. They had everything they needed and were so well-behaved. They were easy to take care of.

Guinea Pigs – Penny, Scout, and Madilyn
They were uneventful—just quiet little cuties. Like the rabbits, they had a great setup and never needed much attention. We'd get feed, water, clean their cage then move on. We always enjoyed taking care of them; they were always so well behaved.

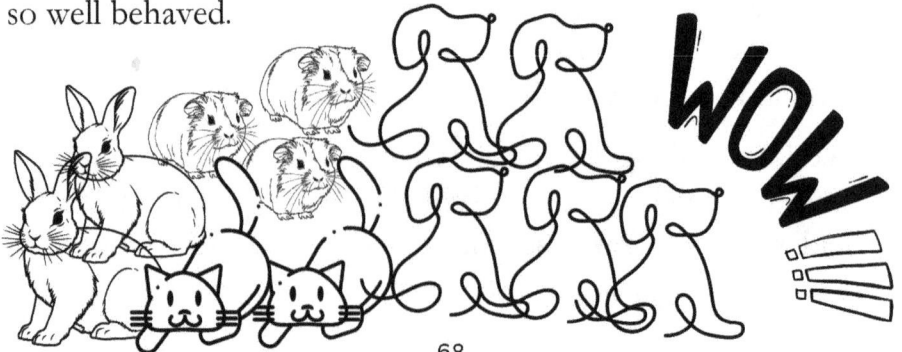

BLIP BLIP BLIP

We did another job that had three guinea pigs. They talked to us—well, we called it talking. They ran around their room going blip blip blip blip—it sounded like bubbles popping.
They were so much fun. We loved taking care of them. They had the greatest setup.

There was a large table with an eight-foot board across it. They had boxes and tubes to run through. There were blankets over the board so it would be soft and comfy for them.
They had food, water, hay—they didn't want for anything. There was a little fence around the edge of the board to keep them in and safe. The blip blip blip was because we were there. It was their way of talking to each other.

If a person is going to own a pet, they must assume the obligation of taking care of that pet—or pets—seriously.
Their people did take their responsibility of caring for the guinea pigs seriously.

We did another job for a lady who had a guinea pig that was as big as a football. This is not an exaggeration—I don't know how he got that big, but he was a sweet boy.
The lady also had a Labrador mix. She and the guinea pig were best friends.

Like the other guinea pigs, he had the best of everything. He lived the good life. But the real fun was letting the guinea pig out and watching him and the dog play. They were so funny!

Living the good life!

SASSY AND SKY

We've gotten dogs ourselves through pet sitting. Sassy was the first. A couple we were sitting for—the man had just gotten off work and was driving home—saw a little dog walking down the railroad track. She was covered in ticks and fleas. So he took her to the vet, thinking he'd get her fixed up and find her a home. But it didn't work out that way. Everyone at home fell in love with her, so he had to keep her.

Then Teresa and I came in. Teresa fell in love with her too. "What's her name?" Teresa asked. "Sassy," he said. "You can take her home with you," he told Teresa. Teresa wanted her, but at the time, we had two big dogs. Sassy was little, and we weren't sure how it would go. We had Shenandoah, a Rhodesian Ridgeback, and Phantom, an Australian Shepherd. So, Sassy stayed with them—until the big dogs passed.

Then she came home with us. Sassy was a Catalan Sheepdog. She was 4 months old when we met her and 7 years old when she came to live with us. We had her for 5 wonderful years—and during that time, we made some great memories. One thing we learned was how she got her name. If you scolded her, she'd listen for a little while... then sass you back! She was so funny. What really got me—she was so smart. I have to say, I believe she was one of the smartest dogs I've ever been around. All dogs are smart, but Sassy was super smart. She just knew things. I have no idea how she understood some of the stuff she did. Sometimes we'd be talking, and she'd shake her head up and down like she was saying "Yes, I got that."

But one day, Teresa and I were joking around. I said something to Teresa, something I knew she'd take as a joke —but still, something she wouldn't care for. And right in the middle of it, Sassy shook her head side to side, like she was saying "No!" Animals know what you're saying when you talk. I already knew that, but Sassy just made it even more clear.

Sassy loved hugs. She would take all the hugs you wanted to give. Hugs and petting—that was her thing. We knew Sassy for 12 years, but the five years she lived with us were the best. It hurt the day she passed. Sassy will never be forgotten. She will live forever in our hearts.

Sweet & Sassy

Then came Sky, an Australian Shepherd. We had lost Sassy just a few months before. A couple we were pet sitting for knew this. One evening, we got a call from them. The story goes: The man was out running when this little dog came up and started running with him. He ran the last mile by his side. After the run, the man went around the neighborhood knocking on doors, asking if anyone knew the dog. Everyone said no. So, he took the little dog home.

The couple called us and told us the story. He was an Australian Shepherd—and that's exactly what we had been looking for. We went to check him out. And guess what? He went home with us. Next up: what do we name him? He was only 4 ½ months old. We came up with the name Sky. We took him to the vet, got him checked out, and just like that —it was time for the three of us to be a family.

We don't know what Sky went through before we met him, but he was something else. He didn't allow us to clean the house. He didn't allow us to use tools to fix things around the house. Anything he thought might hurt you—or someone else—was a no.

But the real thing about Sky was how fast he could change. He could be the sweetest boy one minute… and the next, he would bite. And yes, he did bite. But not because he was mean. It was fear. When he bit, it was because something had scared him.

It was funny in a way—he wouldn't listen to anyone but me. He didn't hear Teresa at all. So, I was the one who took care of him. I fed him, took him out to potty. We had Sky for 11 years. In that time, he and I spent so much time together— we got really close. We got attached.

We became best friends. I'd tell him,
"You're my best buddy."
He'd lay his head on my leg
or lick my face.

When he died,
he took a piece
of me with him.
 I'm happy he did—
we're still connected.
I'll see him again.
Sky, my best buddy.

SKY
MY BEST
BUDDY

LAYLA

We sat for a Boxer named Layla. Nothing was safe from her —if she wanted it, she was going to get it. She was a female tennis ball. If something was up high, she would jump, bounce, climb—whatever it took—until she got it. She even got the TV remote once. We thought, "We'll put it on the mantel—she can't get it there."

Well, the next time we came back, she had the TV remote again!

One day Teresa had an errand to run, so she left me with Layla. Layla and I were playing on the floor, and she hit me in the left temple. I saw stars! Layla had a good right hook.

The couple that had Layla—the man was out of town, and the wife hired us. She and her girlfriends were going out and having fun. But when the man got back, he put a stop to the fun—and to us.

But all was okay. We got to meet Layla, have some laughs, and make some great memories.

LEAVING HIS MARK

Teresa and I are readers. We take books with us everywhere we go. We were on a pet sitting job and had some free time. I had my book out, and Jupiter—the cat we were sitting— walked over and bit it. It has teeth holes in it now.

He bit it and made my book super special. The holes go deep, so he got a good bite. It was so funny. Thankfully, the book was closed when he bit it, so the damage was right in the binding. I still have the book.

MAX AND ELLA

Ella was a Chihuahua. Max was a Chihuahua mix. A girl called and said she had two little dogs and needed pet sitting. Ella was pretty uneventful—she'd bark at you, but once you picked her up, she couldn't love you enough. While we were doing the contract and playing with the dogs, the girl told us Max's story.

Max had been her neighbor's dog, but they kept him tied up outside. She said, "I couldn't handle seeing him tied out like that, so I went over and asked if I could buy him from them."

They told her she could buy him under one condition—if she promised not to change his name. If that was all they wanted—OK! She gave them $60.00 and took Max home with her. From then on, he lived in the house—safe and happy. Ella and Max—two of the sweetest little dogs. They were the best.

LUCY

Lucy was a Standard Poodle. We took Lucy for a walk twice a day. She was great to walk—never had any trouble. She was always a little lady when walking and listened when told to do something. She didn't care much for other dogs; she would just walk by, as long as they didn't bother her.

I took Lucy for her walk one morning and it rained on us. When we got back to Lucy's house, we were good and wet. Someone asked, "What are you two doing all wet?" I said, "Lucy and I were walking, and the sky started leaking."

WALDO BUDDY

Waldo Buddy was a Corgi mix. He was strong-willed and a very busy boy—but you couldn't ask for a sweeter dog. Teresa and I had so much fun running through the house playing with Waldo Buddy.

As for his name: the couple who owned him couldn't agree. The man wanted to name him Waldo, and the woman wanted to name him Buddy—so they compromised and named him Waldo Buddy.

BUDDY

Buddy, a Labrador Retriever was a big, beautiful black dog and a sweet dog who never gave us any trouble. We had to take him for a walk every day. He was so friendly—he had to say hi to everyone, whether it was people we met or other dogs.

HEY BUDDY!

But the one thing that stuck with me was a boy who lived in the neighborhood. He would always come out to the street and talk to me. He said he knew me, but to this day, I have no idea who he was. Buddy liked him though, so I'm sure he was okay. Dogs will let you know if there's trouble in the air. We always had a great time with Buddy. When we'd get back from our walks, Buddy was always ready for more—playing and petting. Buddy never seemed to wear down.

SHANDY AND NOEL

Shandy, a Golden Retriever, was a sweetheart. She loved everyone and never gave anyone any trouble. She loved being petted—if you started petting her, she'd lay there as long as you kept going. Noel, a Miniature Pinscher, was afraid of everything and everybody.

We took them out in the backyard—it was fenced in—but one day, Noel got out of the fence. She ran all over the neighborhood, with us on her trail.

For an hour and a half, we followed her around the neighborhood. Somehow, we finally coaxed her into the garage, then into the house.

PARADISE MOUNTAIN

We did a pet-sitting job that was as close to Heaven on Earth as I think you could get. It was a long drive, but once we got there—it was great. There were two dogs in a pen in the garage. We took them out for their walk and found Paradise Mountain.

The dogs, Teresa, and I stood there looking out—you could see for miles. Nothing but trees, grass, and sky as far as the eye could see. When we walked, the dogs were so sweet and gentle—they never got out of line. We've seen some beautiful places while pet sitting, but this one will live forever in the attic of my mind. I call it Paradise Mountain because it was so peaceful and beautiful.

LINUS

Linus was a Nile Valley Egyptian cat. We sat for a couple who had a unique cat named Linus. They got him when they lived in Egypt. He lived in the garage, and they had a nice setup for him—he had everything he needed. Teresa took care of him, and he thought she was it. Him and her—best friends.

The couple also had two dogs: Lena and Princess. They lived in the house. I took care of them while Teresa saw to Linus. Princess passed away shortly after we started sitting for them. She was older and had a lot of health problems.

Another fun thing—they had feeder boxes on the trees in the backyard for the squirrels. I would fill them every day. As soon as I got back in the house, the squirrels would come around to eat. It was fun to watch them play in the trees and eat the seeds.

JOHNNY CASH

Johnny Cash, a Labrador Retriever loved running in the yard. He lived in a two-story house, and the stairs had a landing halfway up. He loved lying there and getting petted—we did that a lot.

It was so much fun to watch him. We'd lay a treat on his nose, and he'd shake his head. The treat would pop up into the air, and he'd catch it every single time. He never missed. We also took him on long walks. He loved walking around the neighborhood.

KOBE

I told you about Peyton in the first book. Well, there's a new family member now—Kobe. Kobe was a neighborhood cat. Everyone in the neighborhood fed him and helped take care of him. He had it made. But one day, he came to Peyton's and decided to stay.

He's an outside guy. Peyton's family fixed Kobe a nice home outside—he has everything he needs. Summer, winter, rain, or shine—Kobe is home and safe.

When Kobe first moved in, he would run whenever we came to sit. He's gotten better now. I still can't pet him, but he stays nearby when I go in and out of the house. He lets Teresa pet him and even stays with her while she puts out his food and gives him treats. We made a lot of memories with Peyton, and now we're making more with Kobe.

HARVEY

We sat for a girl who fostered puppies from time to time. She had three dogs of her own, but when the animal shelter got full, she would take in a puppy until they could find it a home.

She got one—he was the cutest little guy. His name was Harvey. He had a personality that was over the top. He couldn't love you enough, and he was so funny. You'd tell him to sit—he'd just stand. Tell him to come—he'd turn and go the other way. Tell him to be still—you'd want to take his picture—he'd wiggle! Harvey got a home and went on his way.

DOCTOR COOPER

Dr. Cooper was a Miniature Australian Shepherd. His name was Cooper, but we always called him Dr. Cooper. One day, we were sitting for him. I was walking Cooper in the yard. Teresa was with us but having trouble with her knee. Cooper stopped and looked at her. Then, all at once, he ran and jumped—right into her knee. Oh, the pain of it all!

After he hit her, he just stood there looking at her, and then walked off like nothing had happened. A few minutes later, her knee was fine. From then on, we called him Dr. Cooper.

The funny part? We were at Dr. Cooper's house, talking with his owners. Cooper walked through the room, and his owner said, "That's Dr. Cooper." We thought we were the only ones who called him that!

CHARLIE

Charlie was a Chihuahua. She was so sweet. We only sat for Charlie a few times, but we had so much fun. Charlie lived in an apartment complex. The funny part? Every time we took her for a walk, everyone knew Charlie. Everyone we passed would say, "Hi Charlie! Hi Charlie!" It was so funny—everyone knew her! We just kept thinking, How does everyone here know Charlie? Thinking back, I think I understand now—once you meet Charlie, you never forget her.

SAM AND SNOOP

Sam and Snoop were Collies—outside dogs. Their owners tried to bring them inside, but they didn't want that. They wanted to be outside. They had a great setup: a big building with a doggie door and hay inside so it was warm and comfortable.

Sam and Snoop were so friendly and full of love. Teresa would get their food, I'd get the water. They didn't care much for petting, but Sam loved my singing. I mentioned in the first book that I like to sing while I work.

One morning, I was getting water and started singing. Sam stopped eating, came over, sat down, and looked at me. From then on, I had to sing to Sam every time we sat for them. There was a rock wall, maybe three feet high. I'd sit on it and sing to Sam. He'd lay at my feet.

Snoop's thing was food. He'd take Teresa and show her where the food was, but he wouldn't eat until he got treats first.

It hurt when their owners called and told us Sam had passed away. But we have happy memories.

BAXTER, MIA, AND LULU

Baxter, Mia, and Lulu were three little Yorkies. Baxter was diabetic. We gave him two shots—one in the morning and one in the evening. He was great when it came to his shots —one of the easiest we've ever given.

Mia was a meek little girl. She was so small that if the grass hadn't been mowed, you'd lose her. Lulu stayed in the bedroom on the bed. She was blind, so she didn't move around much.

There was also a cat, Isabella. She was a Himalayan. She didn't care much for socializing, so she stayed in the bedroom with Lulu. They were best friends.

ZOE

Zoe was a white Boxer. She was the sweetest girl you could ever meet. She couldn't love you enough. She had so much energy! I would take her out first thing—she would shoot out of her cage, ready to play. She and I would go through the house in a flash, then outside, around and around the yard, then back in the house.

Teresa always had Zoe's food and fresh water ready. She would eat, and then it was time to play. Don't tell her owner —but the three of us would run through the house: Teresa, Zoe, and myself. We always had a great time together. Zoe grew up and was loose in the house, so she would meet us at the door—that was real fun. We always got excited when we'd get the call to go see Zoe. We knew it was going to be a fun time.

BIX

Bix is a beautiful gray cat. He would sit in a rocking chair and listen to us talk and Teresa read. He was so funny. He would sit and rock—how he made the rocking chair move, I don't know. I've never seen a cat rock in a rocking chair, but he did. That's the thing about pet sitting—it's a fun, happy job.

LITTLE BUNNY AND SNOWFLAKE

Little Bunny and Snowflake were two big rabbits. We had to put on shoe covers before we went in with the bunnies. The bunnies were feisty and quick to get underfoot, especially at mealtime. They were so funny—they would dart in from nowhere. We couldn't pick them up; they would get stressed if handled. We could pet them, but they had to warm up to us first.

We had to give Snowflake medicine after she finished her breakfast and dinner. She was so easy—all you had to do was call her name, and she would come to you and take her medicine. It was so funny — they had like three rooms and a hallway. The owner told us they needed all the rooms because they liked to get away from each other sometimes.

SALLY, HELEN, AND TITAN

We walked Sally every day. She loved her walks—I believe she would've walked for days if you walked with her. She was so gentle and loved to be petted. After her walks, she would go into the bedroom, get on the bed, and we'd go sit with her and pet her. She was not supposed to go upstairs, but she did at times. The funny part was there were only two rooms upstairs. I would go up to get her to come back down, and she would just change rooms—back and forth, with me following behind. It was like a cartoon. Until she finally said, Okay, it's time—let's go downstairs. Sally has passed away, but she left happy memories.

Helen was an outdoor cat. She would come and eat on the front porch and then be gone again. It's funny—even if the pet isn't around all the time, you still get attached. Helen has also passed away.

Then the people got Titan. We don't get to sit Titan—he is his own man, or dog, I guess I should say. He's a pretty dog. We see him and his owner walking around the neighborhood. Pets are funny—they're just like people. They all have their own personalities.

PETS COME FIRST

We sat for a little dog that was getting older. There were steps going into the house, and it was getting hard for the little dog to climb. So, the couple that had the little dog sold the house and bought another that had no steps. Now that is how it should be. Pets come first—you and me, second.

GREENWICH, ONION, DARE, AND REEBOKE

Greenwich was a Dachshund. Onion and Reeboke were Siamese. Dare was an American Shorthair. Onion, Dare, and Reeboke were three pretty uneventful cats—not much went on with them. Onion and Reeboke were brothers. Onion was not nice to Reeboke; he was forever giving him a hard time. Dare was the only girl, and she loved to be petted. She and Teresa petted a lot.

But the story here is about Greenwich. He was a sweet little guy with the most unique markings—he looked like lace. We had never seen a dog with markings like his. He was just so unique. Teresa and I liked Greenwich. He was small, sweet, and had the best personality. He loved everybody and loved to be petted.

We never got to sit for Greenwich. His owner said if we took care of him, we wouldn't give him back. I don't know where she got that, but she said it—so we only got to see him when she was home. We tried hard, but the answer was always no: You wouldn't give him back. That didn't make sense—we would've been sitting for him at her house with the cats. But anyway, people can be funny.

THINGS WE DON'T THINK ABOUT HAPPENING

We all know things happen from time to time that we don't think about happening. They jump up and say, "Hi, I'm here!"

As I've said before, when it comes to pet sitting, we have to go—because the pets come first. I woke up one morning and I was so sick. I don't know what I had or where I got it —just that I don't want it again. Anyway, I started throwing up, but I still had to go. The babies were waiting.

The house we were in only had one bathroom. Teresa was in there, and I felt it coming on. I ran out the front door, and the next thing I knew, I was throwing up in this lady's front yard, with cars going by.

SHADOW, SPARKS, AND KIYA

We had been caring for Shadow. She was a good girl and loved to go for long walks. Then the lady who had Shadow called to say she had a new dog—a friend for Shadow. We went to meet Sparks, a real live wire. The lady was worried how Sparks would do.

As it turned out, we had to go back over to the house after sitting for Shadow and Sparks. The lady was home. We were standing just inside the front door when Sparks came running down the hall, sliding in under our feet. The lady said, "Well, that tells the whole story."

Later, we got a call—Shadow had passed away. The lady said, "I now have Kiya," and like Sparks, Kiya is a ball of fire and a laugh a minute. It's always fun at their house.

HOUSE OF CATS

We do a pet-sitting job at a house that has 16 cats. Talk about a fun time—we have a ball! They have dry food available at all times; they're free-fed. But the real fun begins when Teresa puts out the wet food. Cats come from all directions. Before she can even get all the plates out, they're ready to eat.

Teresa serves the wet food on paper plates. She gets all the plates ready, then sets them down three at a time as fast as she can.

They have several litter boxes. While Teresa is feeding, I clean the potties. One of the little girl cats has taken a liking to me. She stays close, walking all around me as I clean, until the food is ready and Teresa calls her to eat.

We did another house of cats that only had three, but just like the other, we had a routine. It was pretty much the same as with the 16 cats—just on a smaller scale.

DOCTOR BEAR

I told you about Dr. Cooper. As time went by, we met Dr. Bear. We were sitting for Bear, and Teresa's knee was giving her trouble again. She took Bear out and was walking him around the yard.

A day or two later, she told me that Bear had fixed her knee. She said, "We have another doctor!" Dogs make the best doctors.

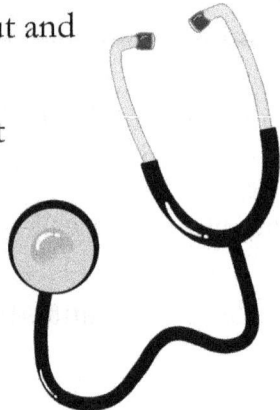

WILD TURKEYS

We went to a job one morning, and when we got there, there were 35 or 40 wild turkeys just walking up the road. We slowed down and went along behind them until we got to the driveway we were going to. When we got out of the car to go inside, the turkeys walked into the yard across the street. When we came back out to leave, they were gone.

GOATS

There was one job we did for a few years that was pretty funny. On the way there, we'd pass a farm that had goats— but they couldn't keep the goats in a fence. The goats would always get out, but they never left the farm. They didn't get out on the road; they just walked around the yard eating grass. The people would gather them up, put them back in the fence... and sure enough, before long, they'd be out again. It became a little joke for us. One of us would say, "The goats are out again," and we'd have a big laugh.

BIRD

We were driving to a job when a bird flew into the front of our car. We didn't think much about it. But when we got to the job, the bird was stuck in the grill of our car. Teresa went into the house to take care of the pets while I dug the dead bird out of the grill. In pet sitting, no two days are the same — and you just never know what tomorrow has in store.

SNOOPY AND BUZZ

Snoopy is a Rat Terrier, and Buzz is a Cockatiel. Snoopy didn't like people as a rule. The man who had him before wasn't kind to him. One day, that man took Snoopy to the veterinarian's office—for what, we don't know. But he never came back.

It turned out the man had passed away, so the veterinarian put Snoopy up for adoption. For some reason, Snoopy liked this one lady right away—they hit it off the moment they met. She had seen Snoopy, found out he was available for adoption, and took him home with her. Snoopy got a great home. He was treated like a prince at her house. He was a smart little guy, too. He could pick out his toys by color. The lady would say, "Go get your red toy," and Snoopy would bring back the red toy. She'd say, "Now get your blue toy," and he'd come back with the blue one. Snoopy was one smart boy.

Then there was Buzz. Buzz just flew into the house one day through an open window. He loved to listen to the Champagne Lady sing. (Norma Zimmer was an American vocalist from The Lawrence Welk Show.) Buzz would sit and listen—and even dance—whenever she sang. Then, one day, Buzz flew right back out the window, just like he came in. That was the last time anyone ever saw him.

TRUCK IN TREES

We started out one morning, driving along — and there it was: a truck in the top of the trees. There were woods down the side of the road, and a pickup truck was about 15, maybe 20 feet up in the treetops. No one was around. Just a pickup truck...in the top of the trees. That will wake you up.

FRANKIE

I told you earlier about sitting for Sir William, Honey Dew, Simba, Frankie, and Edgar. Well, we were sitting for them again—but this story is about Frankie.

We had finished up and had some time before our next job. I was standing in the living room and thought, I've got some time—I'll do a little Tai Chi. I didn't know Frankie was standing beside me.

I started doing a Tai Chi move when, all at once, I heard a cat scream. I looked down, and there was Frankie. She looked up at me, then ran to the back of the house. I don't know what she thought I was doing or what she thought I was going to do to her. I tried to tell her it was okay—I was just doing an exercise.

Frankie and Teresa are best friends. Teresa came in and asked what was wrong. I told her the story. She found Frankie, held her, and let her look out the door—that's their fun thing, and all was good again. Normally Frankie doesn't like to be held—the only one who can do it is Teresa, and only when she lets her look outside. Before we left, I went over and petted Frankie. All was forgiven.

STAR, SCOUT, PUDDIN AND SWEET CHING

Star is an orange and white cat, Scout is a Beagle, Puddin is a Boston Terrier, and Sweet Ching is a black Pug.

Star had only three legs. The couple who had her—the man found her outside his office—took her in. Star had been hurt and was not doing well, so the man took her to the vet's office to get her fixed up and back on her feet. He asked the vet to help find Star a home.

But Star's leg was so badly injured that they had to amputate it. The man continued to check on her, and one day he brought his wife with him. He told her the story of finding Star and explained that he was paying the vet bill, and that the vet would find Star a new home.

But the wife said, "No—she has a home with us." So they took her home. Star got a home. And as they say, she lived happily ever after.

Scout went on long walks with us around the neighborhood. She loved her walks—she could never get enough! At home, she was calm and quiet. We would pet her often; Scout was a well-behaved little dog.

Puddin was a busy little girl. She had only one eye, but you wouldn't know it, watching her get around the house. She didn't have time for petting—she was always on the move.

Then there was Sweet Ching. We didn't sit for her but a few times. She came in after the other babies had passed away. Then the man's job took him, his wife, and Sweet Ching away.

But the one thing they can't take away is the memories of the babies.

THEY'RE NOT HOME

We were unlocking the door at a house. A man across the street was mowing his lawn. Next thing we knew, he was in the driveway on his mower. He said, "They're not home."

"We're the pet sitters," Teresa tells him. "They gave us a key."

I'm thinking: Are we not standing here unlocking the door? Sometimes people just don't think.

There were just two cats. It was pretty uneventful. But then one morning, there were no cats. We went all through the house—it was a big house. They had a lot of places to hide. We went upstairs. No cats. What is going on? Then we saw the attic door open. We went in looking for the cats—and there they were. They were okay. We took them back into the house. All was good again. And yes, we did close the attic door. I knew someone would ask.

PEACEFUL SLEEP

When a pet lays down beside me and goes to sleep, I know I've done my job. I want pets to feel at peace with me. I pride myself on this—nothing brings a bigger smile to my face or makes me happier than seeing a pet peacefully sleeping beside me.

ZODI

We only sat for Zodi, a Boston Terrier, a few times, but she is one little dog you never forget. There's one move Zodi made that neither we nor her owner will ever forget. Teresa and I weren't sitting for Zodi that day—her owner had taken her along while running some errands.

They were driving down a busy main street with businesses and restaurants. The girl told us they were stopped at a red light in front of a fast food restaurant. The passenger-side window was down so Zodi could get some fresh air. But as soon as the car stopped at the light, Zodi jumped out the window and ran straight to the fast food restaurant!

The girl said when she finally got the car turned around and made it to the restaurant, Zodi was already sitting with some construction workers who were having lunch at an outdoor table. They were talking to Zodi and sharing bits of their food with her. It was a great ending to a scary moment—and thankfully, Zodi didn't hurt herself when she jumped out of the car.

CHUNK

Chunk, an English Bulldog, was only 13 weeks old. Do you know how much energy a little guy like that has? His owner told Teresa that Chunk couldn't run. That was not true. That little guy could move. Teresa took him out to potty. I started out the door, and Chunk came running across the back deck —believe me, he was moving, with Teresa right behind him trying to catch him!

That's pet sitting for you. Most of the time, what the owners told us about how the pet would act turned out to be the opposite.

BENTLEY

We only sat for Bentley, a Pit Bull, for about a year or so. His owners asked us to check on him—they didn't want him home alone all day. He had cancer, but you would've never guessed it by looking at him or by the way he acted.

He was so funny. He really took up with Teresa and me. And if his owners were off from work and Teresa and I didn't come, he would get upset and act out. It drove his owners crazy! We would take him out in the yard for a run—his idea. Bentley didn't walk. He ran everywhere.

It was a sad day when Bentley passed away, but he left us with a lot of happy memories.

SOLO, BAILEY, AND SCOTTY

Solo was a Saint Bernard mix who loved apples. There was an apple tree in the backyard where we took Solo to potty. Solo would go across the yard and get himself an apple to eat.

Bailey was a Lhasa Apso. She was pretty uneventful—a quiet girl. Bailey felt it was her job to take care of the house, and she would alert everyone if anyone came around.

Solo got sick and passed away. Then in came Scotty, a Terrier mix. He was a rescue and had been abused, so he was cautious —but he would take a treat right out of your hand.

PEBBLES, BAM BAM, GRACIE, LUCKY, SHESHE, CHI-CHI, ELEAKNOIR, AND XANDER

We sat for Pebbles first. At the start, it was just him and his owner. Pebbles was pretty uneventful, but I'll give him this —he was 19 years old, so yes, he was moving slow. Then Pebbles' owner got married, and they got Bam Bam and Gracie. They were sweet cats, like Pebbles—uneventful but nice.

Then Lucky came in, and things livened up. He was a ham— he loved to be petted. He would come over and fall right over, wanting you to pet his belly. When we took him out to potty, we'd run around the yard and have a ball. But when we went back inside, things didn't stop there. Lucky just kept going—he was a ball of fun. Then Lucky got old, and his health started failing. It was a sad day when we heard Lucky had passed away.

The job also had two guinea pigs—Sheshe and Chi-Chi. They were fun. Teresa took care of them and would always tell me the funny things they did.

There were also two goldfish. The people really took care of their pets—they had to! I've never seen goldfish that big in a home aquarium.

Then a baby kitty named Eleaknoir came along. Eleaknoir was just 8 months old when we met her. At that time, it was just Eleaknoir and Gracie left—the other babies had passed away, except for one of the goldfish. Gracie kept to himself; we didn't see him much. But Eleaknoir stayed close. She liked petting. The first couple of trips, she was unsure and kept to herself, but by the third trip, she was all over us— petting, climbing, walking on us. By then, Teresa was petting Gracie too, and by the third trip, everything was cool.

One morning something fun happened. I went to clean the potties, and Gracie was standing and looking at me. I bent over and said, "Come here, I'll pet you." He walked up to me, and we petted for a few minutes. Then, as pets do, he got his eye on something else and off he went.

And then there's Xander. Now he is one sweet cat. He's an outside cat but has everything he needs—a house to get in and out of the weather, food and water, and all the petting you can ask for. Every time someone goes in or out the door, Xander gets some petting. Truthfully, he's the neighborhood cat. He goes all around, and everyone knows him, but he stays at the house where we pet sit most of the time.

Oh, one last thing—I'd never seen this before, but when Teresa fed the goldfish, she would shell green peas (frozen and thawed), then shell them, and feed them to the goldfish. You can't go wrong with pets—they make life, life.

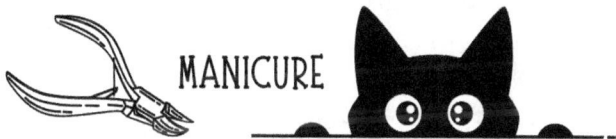

MANICURE

We were on a job. Teresa was feeding a cat. I heard her say, "You need your nails trimmed." She got her clippers—she always carries them just in case—and started trimming the cat's nails. The little cat wasn't thrilled, but didn't give her much trouble.

But the funny part? Teresa had trimmed three paws. Then she went to trim the last paw, she was holding it in her hand. Suddenly, the little cat took one of its other paws and covered the paw Teresa was holding. I had to laugh—it was so funny. Teresa moved the paw and finished the trim. No one was hurt, and the little cat felt good after her manicure.

BAILEY

Bailey was a Corgi/Jack Russell Mix. It was so funny the first time we sat for Bailey. When we went into the house, he didn't know us. We had only met him once before, and it had been a while. When he saw us, he started howling—he sounded like a house alarm! He didn't remember us at first, but it only took a few minutes, and we were all friends again.

Everywhere we went in the house, Bailey was right there with us. I didn't know at the time that Bailey was almost blind. He could see shadows and shapes, but watching him, you wouldn't have guessed it. I only found out when Teresa told me.

There were cats at the house, and Bailey loved to bark at them. He didn't do anything—just bark. Most of the time, he would just walk right by them. When Teresa took him out to potty, he would bark at other dogs too. That was just his thing. It would be great to see Bailey again. He was a cool little guy.

BUTTERMILK, SMOKEY, SEYMORE, AND PUMPKIN

They were four sweet cats. Buttermilk loved to be petted—she would stay petted as long as you would keep going. Smokey liked petting a little. She wasn't big on the petting department, but a little is better than none. Seymore was the only boy. He kept to himself. He would come to eat but no petting for him. Pumpkin was the funny one. Every time we would go to leave, Pumpkin would be lying on top of our car. We'd come out, and there she'd be—on the roof of our car. We always got a big laugh out of her.

SASHA AND LITTLE BIT

Sasha and Little Bit were two Pit Bulls. We only sat for them once, but we will never forget them. They were so loving— you couldn't ask for sweeter dogs. Their cages didn't have bottoms, and we never understood why, but Sasha and Little Bit didn't seem to mind. They were just happy and gentle souls.

GINGER, KIKI, BIRDS, AND HENRY

Ginger was a little black dog and the most active little girl. Teresa and I would take her out—she loved to run in the backyard. She would just go wild running and playing ball. We played ball until we told her it was time to go in and take care of the other babies. Ginger would stop and walk into the house —no problem.

Kiki was a beautiful cat. She was funny—she'd pet you, but you didn't pet her.

There were also 10 cinnamon finches. They were birds and no trouble, but they didn't do much. Birds are pretty easy and pretty to care for.

Then there was Henry, the turtle. Henry lived in an aquarium tank on the back of the toilet. He didn't do much, but we would go in and talk to him, give him a little food—just to keep him company.

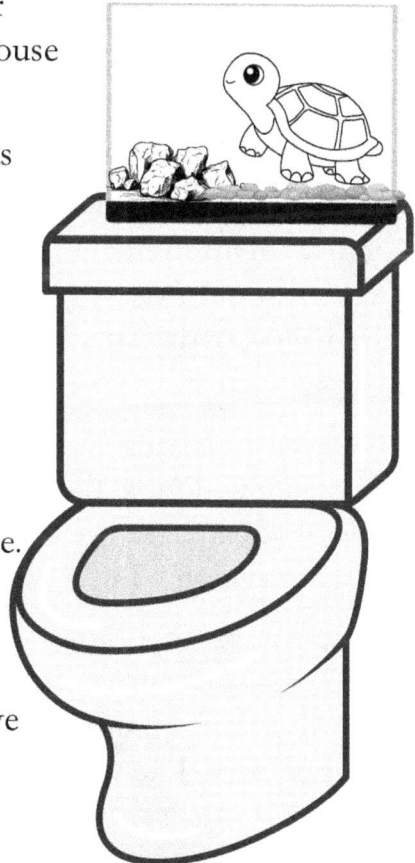

COVID

Hey, remember COVID-19, the big bad pandemic? When everything came to a standstill—well, most everything.
They closed office buildings, locked down nursing homes, no visitors—no one could check on loved ones except by phone.

I remember some people went and stood outside the window and talked to their mom or dad or grandparent—whoever was in there. And that worked for the family and the person they came to see. You did what you had to do.
Life was turned upside down. Life just changed overnight. The only thing we could do was handle it

The thing was, for Teresa and me, life went on. We had some cancellations, but as you've read, we had what we called lunch runs. The people we sat for during the lunch runs got to keep working, so we still had work and money coming in—a blessing at that time.

The wild thing was, we were still getting contracts. Yes, we got new clients in the middle of the pandemic.
We put on our masks, grabbed our hand sanitizer, and went to work every day. It was down to half a day, but we were working.

The biggest blessing was Teresa or I never got sick. We did the isolation during the pandemic as best we could. The babies had to have food and water. Dogs still had to be taken out to potty. Litter boxes had to be cleaned.

The universe was good to Teresa and me during the pandemic—we still worked, made some money, never stopped working, put money in the bank, and paid our bills. Never got sick. Life was good. It was tight, but good.

The only thing was, in between jobs, we had to stay home. Other than the bank and grocery store, we went nowhere. Not getting to celebrate holidays with family meant nothing in pet sitting. We never got to celebrate holidays on the day of—they were always days before or days after, never on the day. But it's okay—you get it in there. As I have learned, holidays and weekends are when you make your money in pet sitting.

WIND CHIMES

A client called to set up pet sitting. When I answered the phone, all I could hear were wind chimes. Never had that happen before—but it was great. The client started talking, with the wind chimes ringing behind her. It was so cool.

As a joke, I called her the next morning and said, "Don't call us again unless you're out with the wind chimes." She told me that made her day.

Wind chimes are peaceful. They bring a calm feeling. I didn't know for a long time that wind chimes have spiritual meaning. They promote peace and reduce stress.

The client has a little dog we sit for. It's always fun taking her out and playing in the backyard—with the wind chimes singing. But now... even more so.

BAILEY AND COSMO

Bailey was a Cocker Spaniel and Cosmo a Chihuahua. Bailey was a pretty uneventful girl—just a little sweetheart who loved to be petted. Cosmo has a bigger story. He was abused.

The girl who had Bailey and Cosmo also had a young son— maybe 12 or 13. He had some friends he'd stay with on weekends. They had this little dog, Cosmo. Those boys abused him all the time. When Cosmo would go to eat, they'd pick at him and not let him eat. They never petted him—just picked on him and roughed him up.

But the way Cosmo came to live with the woman and her son we sat for—that was Cosmo's idea.
One morning, she went to pick her son up. When he got in the car, Cosmo jumped in with him—and refused to get out. So the people told them, "Take him." Cosmo had moved out on his own.

He was the sweetest little guy. I don't understand how anyone could abuse or mistreat him—but he chose the right home. He was treated like a king. He never had to worry about food again. He had a big yard to run and play in—and a big sister named Bailey. Bailey and Cosmo became best friends the minute they met.

DAISY

Daisy was a sweet little dog. She loved playing ball. Teresa and I played a lot of ball with her in the backyard. She needed daily exercise, so we made sure she got it. We only sat for Daisy one week, but we will never forget her. Some dogs, you don't have to know long—they stay with you forever.

READING TO ANIMALS

I told you about Teresa and me reading to the pets. I never thought of reading to animals, but most dogs and cats like being read to. And it's funny—they will let you know if they like what you are reading. They will sit and listen, and sometimes even go to sleep.

And if they don't like what you're reading, they will leave. What's funny is cats like dog stories and dogs like cat stories most of the time. Occasionally, you'll get a cat that will listen to cat stories or a dog that will listen to dog stories.

I just learned if a child has trouble with reading, have them read to animals—dogs, cats, birds. The animals enjoy it, and over time, it will help with reading troubles. If you have a pet in your home, great. If not, you can go to an animal shelter.

Like I said, this not only helps the child, but it's good for the pets as well. And you don't have to be a kid—adults can also read to animals. You can volunteer at an animal shelter as well. You don't have to have trouble with reading; just read for your pets. Teresa and I are not kids, and we read to pets most every day.

TERESA'S RULES

Teresa had rules.

One was:
thirty minutes—you stayed
with the pets thirty minutes per job.
If they were alone, we would stay longer
to give them some company.

Another rule:
no mistreating a pet.
One time, and you were out.
No questions asked.

Another rule:
the pets always came first.
If we felt bad or were sick,
we always saw to the pets first,
then ourselves.
Teresa had a Do Not Sit list.
Once you got on the list, you never got off.

BALLET

I love ballet it's the greatest art ever.
The great thing about pet sitting.
I have ballet all year round.
I call it Nature's Ballets.

NATURE'S BALLETS

Spring:
Flowers bloom and dance in the wind.

Summer:
Rain dances Ballet as it hits the ground.

Fall:
Multi-colored leaves dance in the wind
as they fall to the ground.
Multi-colored leaves dance across
the ground in the wind.

Winter:
Snowflakes dance a beautiful Ballet
as they fall to earth.

Then It's Spring Again:
the dogwood trees bloom
and give us Tutu trees.

ACKNOWLEDGMENTS

A big thank you to Teresa—she made all this possible. Thank you to author Jeni Brown; without her expertise, the books would never have been written. Thank you to veterinarian Vicky Owens McGrath for the wonderful foreword she wrote.

Truly Grateful for you.

ABOUT THE AUTHOR

Garry White is the author of *Stories From Mama's Babies Pet Sitting*. He had a ghost story he wrote published in the book *More True Tales of Ghosts, Spirits, and Angels* by author Thomas Lee Freese.

Make All The Earth
A Place Of Peace
For All Pets And Animals.

www.ingramcontent.com/pod-product-compliance
Lightning Source LLC
Chambersburg PA
CBHW060336050426
42449CB00011B/2766